Everyone Remembers the Elephant in the Pink Tutu

How to Promote and Publicize Your Business with Impact and Style

By
Mary Maloney Cronin
&
Suzanne Caplan

W0007964

CAREER PRESS
3 Tice Road, P.O. Box 687
Franklin Lakes, NJ 07417
1-800-CAREER-1
201-848-0310 (NJ and outside U.S.)
Fax: 201-848-1727

EVERYONE REMEMBERS THE ELEPHANT IN THE PINK TUTU
Cover design by Hub Graphics
Printed in the U.S.A. by Book-mart Press

To order this title, please call toll-free 1-800-CAREER-1 (NJ and Canada: 201-848-0310) to order using VISA or MasterCard, or for further information on books from Career Press.

Library of Congress Cataloging-in-Publication Data

Cronin, Mary Maloney.
    Everyone remembers the elephant in the pink tutu : how to promote
and publicize your business with impact and style / by Mary Maloney
Cronin & Suzanne Caplan.
        p.   cm.
    Includes index.
    ISBN 1-56414-360-0 (pbk.)
    1. Advertising.   2. Small business.   I. Caplan, Suzanne.
    II. Title.
    HF5823.C74   1998   98-4096
    659.1--dc21

Dedications

··

To my grandmothers Mary Catherine Maloney and Elizabeth T. Torres.

—MMC

To Betty Caplan Liff. More than family, a treasured friend.

—SC

Acknowledgments

Mary Maloney Cronin would like to thank:

My savvy agent, Laurie Harper of the Sebastian Agency in San Francisco, for her moxie, integrity, and sound business advice. You're a real pro and my savior.

I'd also like to thank: my co-author, Suzanne Caplan, for gifting me with the title of this book and her writing skills, and for introducing me to Laurie; Ron Fry and Michael Gaffney of Career Press—both were instrumental in the launching of the Tutu concept; my media friends and colleagues who served as interviewees and provided insight, offered quotable quotes, and read the manuscript to ensure its accuracy; my clients and Cronin Communications' business associates for their enthusiasm and support of this project; my mastermind team for guiding me through tough decisions and for helping me to turn work into an incredibly valuable adventure.

Saying thank you to my family and friends somehow seems inadequate. My heartfelt appreciation will never waver for my parents,

John and Mary Frances Maloney; my brothers Sean and Patrick, and Patrick's wife Mary Ellen; my sisters Meghan, Mary Frances, and Maria Theresa; my partner in life, Chris Cronin, and his family; my lifelong and dear friends, particularly Corina Benner and Suzanne Sliker; and of course, my buddies Timer and Louis for burning the midnight oil with me, purring away. I swear they're cheering me onward!

Suzanne Caplan would like to thank:

My agent Laurie Harper for years of a working relationship that works. Sherry Truesdell, the database wonder for maintaining the manuscript in organized form as always. And my normal cast of characters: Jean Hunter, Paul Mason, Norm Belt, Mark Bibro, Debbie and Don Phillips, and Jeff Cowan for all that they have meant to my life and my work.

Contents

....

Introduction

The 100th birthday of a hospital in a conservative small town outside of Philadelphia is not exactly an earth-shattering event. On the sizzle and sex appeal chart, it's a no-show. Not thought of as a natural for a public relations campaign.

Yet, driven by the enthusiasm of a young and very motivated PR professional, the promotion turned out to be a gigantic success. The young publicist was Mary Maloney and her concept was a "Great Baby Birthday Party." With little money and skeptical support from the hospital board, Mary and her fellow department associates sent out makeshift fliers through every outlet they could find within the hospital and community. The fliers featured an invitation to a birthday party and a request for all individuals born at the hospital to register for a special gift.

The flier, along with a press release, was sent to the media. Then, friendly but consistent (and persistent) follow-up was employed. Mary's enthusiasm about the event soon spread to the PR staff, the respondents to the invitation, and the media, as well. The reluctant hospital management finally got caught up in the excitement.

The expected 500 replies turned into 7,500 registrations from 30 states. People well into their 90s were sending four-page letters describing what it was like growing up near the hospital. One couple sent a note of thanks to the nurses who helped get them through the birth of their triplets. And others just sent messages of greetings. The party included a cake 12 feet high and 8 feet wide and almost 2,000 people were there to blow out the candles. The hospital received coverage on *Good Morning America* and the story was picked up on the wire services, spreading quickly to major newspapers and periodicals throughout the country. Years later, people still talk about the "Great Baby Button," the special gift given to everyone who registered.

This is what great PR is all about: an idea, well-positioned and well-executed. Why was this event so successful in attracting media attention? Because it was wearing a pink tutu! Let me explain: You've heard it said before that when a dog bites a man, it's not news—but when a man bites a dog, *that's* news. A business that sends out a flurry of press releases about ordinary occurrences, everyday news, and uneventful events will not get much play in the news. So, if you're an entrepreneur, a businessperson, or responsible for getting publicity for your company, you want to release information that will attract media attention, like the story of a man biting a dog. You want your efforts to stand out in a crowd.

The problem today is that the *crowd* is getting more crowded. It's a competitive economy, no matter what your business, product, or service. And you can bet that your competitors are equally interested in getting that news coverage and air time. You're not just dealing with a *crowd* here—you're dealing with a crowd of elephants! So how do you set yourself apart from the rest of the herd? Try a pink tutu.

In this book, we refer to the elephant in a pink tutu as a metaphor for good public relations and publicity efforts. After all, if you came across a line of 100 gray elephants and saw that one of them was wearing a pink tutu, which one would you be curious about? Which one would you remember? They're all elephants—one is just packaged in bright colors.

And this is what this book is about as well—how to take what may seem like an ordinary event, product, or service and turn it into an attention-getter. We offer a complete approach to learning the best ways to get your company, product, or service into the media spotlight. You will learn how to identify your "hook" and how to position yourself with the media so that you get maximum and favorable coverage. You will discover when to use a press release and when a full media kit is necessary—and we will help you create both. You will find tips on effective follow-up to your mail campaigns to make sure your story gets to the top of the pile. You will read about strategies to ensure that your interviews and media coverage accomplish the results you want. And finally, you will explore advice that will get you through a media crisis. (Of course, we hope that bad publicity is something you never have to encounter—but it never hurts to be prepared.)

Whether you are a freelancer, a consultant, an established business owner, or a new entrepreneur, this book will help guide you through the PR process so crucial to any business success. Within these pages, you will discover how to find your own tutu and get out and dance.

Read on and find out how you can become a stand-out!

Chapter 1

What to expect at the circus

Getting to Know the Media

The bright lights of the media can be as dazzling as a three-ring circus, and as intimidating as the dangerous animals performing in the center ring. The media are powerful, unpredictable—and not fully understood by those who don't control them. If you can successfully harness the power and focus of the media positively on yourself and your venture, your efforts may result in show-stopping attention for your company.

But if you're poorly prepared to approach the media, your results may be as disastrous as sticking your head into the mouth of an untamed lion. You may find yourself on the receiving end of negative public attention, which may end in a disaster with long-lasting effect. This risk is the primary reason that few smaller companies begin a PR campaign at all.

The payoff is sufficient to make the risk worth taking, and you can increase the odds in your favor if you know what to expect. The key is to understand the needs of the media; respect the demands of filling the pages and the airwaves with interesting, accurate, and relevant information, and appreciate the relentless time pressures facing most workers in the field.

Armed with this information, you can be the beneficiary of thousands of dollars worth of free advertising that will result in awareness and increased demand for your products or services.

Begin by clearing up your misconceptions

The mystique that surrounds the press creates assumptions that are not true in whole or in part. Let's debunk a few of them.

Misconception #1: The media won't cover stories on a startup business. The *age* of a business does not determine whether it is of interest to the press. In fact, if you are starting a very new and unique venture, that fact may be just what fires up the imagination and interest of the press. Or perhaps the hook is the way you went about starting your business or the hurdles you had to overcome. At a time when you need PR the most, you really might be able to get it if you take the time to present a special aspect of your story to the press.

Misconception #2: If I just send out information, the media will call me. Fact is, if your story is incredible enough, this might happen. But chances are it won't. The media is inundated with press releases and phone calls, many of them similar to yours. Therefore, your work must continue after the information is sent.

In these pages, you will learn what it takes to make your initial contact and, more important, how to follow through. If you refuse to be daunted by an initial lack of response, you and your perseverance will get you the attention that you want and deserve.

Misconception #3: The stories I place will generate a ton of business for me. In the very rarest of circumstances, a great story will result in the phone ringing off the hook with potential new clients or buyers. But this doesn't happen often enough to count on. What *will* happen with several well-placed and positive stories about you and your business is that a valuable aura of credibility will surround your company. People will remember your name and perhaps the nature of your business. This paves the way for you to follow up with your sales and marketing efforts, giving you a solid base from which to grow your company.

If you are marketing to business or corporate clients, a track record of press coverage may translate into marketing material. Copy the best articles and send them to your customers and clients.

Misconception #4: The media always sensationalizes stories to attract readers. The media is not a one-size-fits-all industry—it varies from the serious journalistic ventures of daily print and broadcast news to the tabloid papers and TV shows. The average business story is of little interest to TV, and serious journalists are looking for genuine and interesting information for their readers or listeners. You won't target the sensational press with your releases and attention so it is unlikely that they will target you.

Misconception #5: The media can't be trusted—they never get it right. Most of the media will do everything they can to get it right. After all, their reputation is on the line as well. But they must rely on their sources to give them accurate and complete information. This means *you*. Before you agree to be interviewed, make sure you have all of your facts and are prepared to answer all of the questions that may be posed. Scrambling for information at the last minute and being unsure of the answers to questions are surefire ways to make the things you say "not quite right" when you see it in print.

Good reporters aspire to inform their readers; if they can't get the facts and details from you, they may contact other sources—and the story may take a slant that doesn't put you in the best light.

On the other hand, don't think that you can set out to embellish a story and deceive your interviewer. You may end up with a very unflattering story.

Researching media outlets

If you wanted to be hired for a job, the first thing you would do is find out something about the company you are considering. Use the same technique with media you hope will provide publicity for you.

♦ Learn as much as you can about the station or publication.

♦ Understand the specific philosophy and mission of the media source you're approaching.

♦ Know the key players and their roles.

♦ Read or listen to the media source in order to learn the personality of the organization.

♦ When you have a meeting with a representative of that media source, be on time and have all the necessary information with you.

♦ Be prepared to answer all of the questions that might come up. Role-play with a friend or mentor in advance.

♦ Send a thank you note for any meeting or interaction. Be polite and courteous.

The best jobs come from a focused approach and the best interviews start the same way. Before you even approach a member of the press, take the time to make sure that you are sending it to the right person in the right organization.

If you are aware of a media source but aren't completely familiar with it, call to get a media kit. Loaded with demographic information intended for advertisers, these kits will clearly give you a snapshot of the type of people and the geographical areas this media outlet serves. Print media kits will include a sample copy of the publication. Read it and learn about the reporters and their areas of interest. What is the editorial focus? Does the publication have a short feature section that would be perfect for a piece about you? Does it cover small business?

For the broadcast media, start by watching or listening to the program. Radio and TV stations have media kits as well. If you have questions, it's generally possible to speak to a program representative to get answers. Once you're comfortable with the goals, topics, and direction that a particular program takes, then you may be ready to pitch your story.

There are unwritten rules—learn them

Once you've been interviewed for a story, you shouldn't expect the reporter or editor to allow you or your company the opportunity to review the piece before it goes to print or on the air. You may be understandably nervous about how you look or what you say. You may want one last chance to correct any errors. But editorial custom will rule this out and you will have to wait until the actual story is released.

However, if there is a glaring inaccuracy, most media members will allow you to go on the record with a correction. You've seen clarifications printed in your local paper and even retractions made on the air. If the matter is small, perhaps you should let it rest—but feel free to make a point over a major discrepancy in facts.

The second unwritten rule is that *you* don't have any control over the editorial calendar. Each day there are a number of stories (and reporters) competing for space or air time. Everyone wants their story in a featured space such as the Sunday magazine. But these decisions are made solely by the editor. Even the reporter who worked on the story may have little say-so. Understand that you will have virtually none at all. In the end, you might be surprised at how many people read the back page or listen to the 7 a.m. news.

The media are on a busy schedule

Like most jobs today, working in any area of the media is high-stress business. Reporters, editors, and producers are faced with all of the day-to-day tasks of dealing with people who want their attention, completing their current story assignments and developing new story ideas. And they do this under constant deadline pressure. Each day, the most well-planned schedule may be thrown off because of a breaking story. Then it's back to the drawing board with even less time to complete the work.

Your understanding and respect for these demands will make the jobs of those you work with easier. And the respect that you establish may result in a valuable media contact for your future.

The print media receives stacks of mail every day containing press releases, far more than they can ever use. Many who review such mail use a system for sorting it by reading the heading and then perhaps the first paragraph. If the article doesn't catch their attention, the release gets pitched. However, some releases may be kept for future reference in specific columns such as "Business Notes," "People on the Move," or "Calendar Listings." If you know that your story or event will fit into one of these sections, put it on the top of the release. It will increase the odds of your going to print at some point.

They'll say yes and they'll say no

One of the exciting aspects about the media is also one of the most nerve-wracking and frustrating—you're never quite sure *if* your story will run. Not just *when,* but *if.*

Situations beyond your control may occur at just the time that your story was scheduled. Think of all the great items that were bumped when the Gulf War broke out. It may be a giant unexpected storm, a devastating accident, or a sensational crime. You should always think positively but never be totally surprised if the forces of nature don't cooperate with you on your day. There will be other chances. A poor-sport attitude may work against you, so keep your disappointment to yourself.

The media need you and you need them

In the wake of Princess Diana's death, much was made over the *paparazzi* and, even, the more aggressive photo journalists. In the end, however, it had to be acknowledged that the relationship between celebrity and photographer is mutually beneficial. For those who make their careers in the public, the press is a necessary component. For those who want to raise the public awareness about themselves and their company, the press is a valuable commodity. The fact that Donald Trump lives a very public life is only partially driven by his ego. He knows that a high profile for him and his name translates into business for his hotels and casinos.

He feeds the press and they feed him. And make no mistake about how much he needs a ready supply of new—and often controversial—stories to keep his name in the news.

If you can prove to be the material for newsworthy and compelling stories, you will find yourself in demand. Local and even national press will come to rely on you to give them a good quote or a good angle on their current story idea.

Chapter 2

What color is your tutu, really?

The Importance of the Truth—and Nothing but the Truth

Most members of the mainstream media are committed to ensuring the accuracy of any story they run. They know that they may be held liable for any false information that they print, particularly if it does damage to an individual or a business.

Take caution here to understand that whenever you do business with a friend, you must keep arms length in mixing your personal/professional dealings—not to do so, in some cases, would be risky for you both. And when it comes to a friend in the media, the goal is the story. Anything you want to be kept confidential, you should keep to yourself. Other than this caveat, your relationship with the media can be a mutually beneficial and friendly one.

Start with a win-win philosophy

A good story about your company in any media format—newspapers, magazines, newsletters, radio, TV, or the Internet—will heighten public awareness about you and your product or service. The media will benefit by providing interesting information for their readers or listeners, increasing their circulation or market share.

Let's look at how both of you will win:

For You	For the Media
You establish a memorable identity for your company.	They demonstrate their support of the local community and its businesses.
You get free exposure!	They find a potential new advertiser.
You attain instant credibility.	They provide candid, insightful reporting.
You are positioned as expert or authority.	They find a source to call on for future stories.
You can use the stories in overall marketing effort.	They can sell reprints, which help to promote their publication.
Media coverage adds a mystique to your business that makes it desirable.	Their story adds a quality to their publication that attracts more loyal readers/listeners.

Always put a premium on honesty

Initially, you may be overly concerned about how you will be represented in any story, and it would be natural to try to protect yourself with a bit of positive exaggeration. After all, you want to be seen as knowledgeable, professional, and successful. So why not add an extra college degree or pad the revenue of your business? This temptation may be understandable, but it is highly discouraged.

First of all, any careful reporter who has the time will do some independent fact-checking. If your misstatements are exposed by independent research, your credibility will go down to zero—and your dishonesty may be the spotlight of any story that appears. Little else that you say will be believed and any future possibilities will be over unless, of course, it's an exposé about your further misdeeds. An angry reporter is a powerful adversary—don't create one.

Don't be greedy

If you have begun to develop a good public relations campaign and have seen the positive results on your business, you may think more is better. And perhaps it is. But unless you are doing something that is constantly newsworthy, the media won't be interested. And as you are building your PR, you will be developing more personal relationships as well. Don't jeopardize these by demanding that your name, face, or product be covered constantly. The media must maintain their own objectivity. Being seen as your private agent would have a negative impact on a reporter's credibility and career.

Respect time demands—don't cry wolf

Along the same lines as not asking for an inordinate amount of coverage from those you know personally, don't bombard the general media with junk press releases. If there is something genuinely newsworthy happening, by all means send it out. But don't fall into the trap of issuing releases all the time in the hopes that one will sift through the pack. Any reporter or editor who sees your name on an ongoing basis—usually attached to a very mundane, self-serving press release—will start to tune out after a while and not read anything you send. The volume of press releases is such that reporters have to be discerning.

Evan Pattak, former editor of the monthly *Executive Report Magazine*, local to Pittsburgh, Pennsylvania, reports that he received between 200 and 300 press releases each week. "Ninety percent of them weren't usable," Pattak reports, explaining that this is primarily because the information wasn't suited to his audience. He says he was amazed by how many releases he received from out of state, clearly unsuitable for a publication reporting on local business news.

Let's assume that it takes two minutes to read the average press release and digest its contents. Three hundred releases could take 600 minutes. That's 10 hours—or more than one full day to review! No wonder an efficient editor learns shortcuts to handle this volume.

Send a release only when you have a story—don't cry wolf. If you do, you may find the result is as it was in the fairy tale—you won't get coverage for a real event when it occurs.

Be as accessible as possible

Your work may be very demanding and your schedule hectic, but your deadlines are likely not as rigid as the ones the media establishes. In the early stages of story development, your contact may have some flexibility with time but when it comes down to crunch time—going on air or going to print, the pressure is on. You may have to give follow-up information or clarification. If you can't be reached, the story may have to run without it or, worse yet, not run at all.

It is always good business practice to take media phone calls. Return them promptly and get back to callers with the information or answers that you promise. For good relations with the media, these cardinal rules of good business behavior should be scrupulously followed.

Don't be surprised if your past is exposed

If the real reason that you are so interesting is that you have a controversial past (or present), perhaps you need to keep a low profile. From time to time you'll see an embattled public figure, in politics or business, with a tough legal problem, take to the air hoping that his or her voice will be the loudest one heard and drown out the criticism. It rarely works—there is always one tenacious reporter who won't be silenced.

Most likely you don't have the time, the talent, or the contacts to make a good adversary for the ambitious media. So if there are skeletons in your closet, maybe you should stay behind the doors, as well.

Isn't any press good press?

There's an old adage that it doesn't matter what they say about you as long as they spell your name right. Perhaps for the more flamboyant businesses, such as night clubs, casinos, or anything entertainment-related, that may be true. But for most enterprises, positive media coverage is the only type that will serve your business well.

Chapter 3

What a lovely plaid tutu you have!

How to Set Yourself Apart

Every individual is different. Even within the same family, there are no interchangeable people. Height, weight, color of hair, shape of face, etc.—all of these are distinguishing features. Not to mention personality traits, personal habits, hobbies, interests, and emotional makeup. Your image, just like the elephant's tutu, can be any color you want to make it—just make sure you choose one that flatters.

Every *company* is different, as well. The contrast may be found in the size, the location, the way it delivers its products and services. Even the personality of the owner or manager manifests itself in the way the company operates.

Most of us have worked hard to *eliminate* our differences, trying to fit in. We wear the official "uniform" to work, search for jobs with the properly formatted resumes and cover letters, and prepare to answer interview questions with the expected "right" answers. But when it comes to capturing the attention of potential customers, we must try another strategy—we must play up our *differences* to make us stand out.

Even if your primary business is one that seems very ordinary or is in a field crowded with competitors—there is one (or perhaps a few) unique hooks that you can build a PR campaign around. You just have to find them.

Take, for example, the business of selling fast food—hamburgers to be specific. The product is fairly standard, the restaurants virtually look the same and they're all located along the major roads and highways. So if you were looking for a way to make your fast-food chain stand out in your market, what would you do?

How about choosing an ordinary looking, soft-spoken, middle-aged man to be your spokesperson? Surely *this* choice would be doomed to obscurity because it simply isn't interesting enough. Wrong!! Just look at the character of Dave Thomas, founder of Wendy's, and follow how the use of his image has helped to make this fast-food chain a growing success.

At first thought, maybe you can't identify exactly what it is that has captured the interest of the media, but you will acknowledge that Wendy's has done just that. Although the company has a huge advertising budget, it is the more human side of Dave Thomas that the media has revealed. Thomas' difficult childhood, rise from poverty, and even his 1997 coronary bypass surgery made the news. When this event was covered along with the questions about hamburgers, cholesterol, and coronary artery disease, Wendy's quickly responded with an all-out promotion of their healthier chicken products.

What is it that is so interesting about Dave Thomas? Most of us would not expect someone who seems so ordinary to be as wealthy, powerful, and successful. The public tends to relate to Thomas on a very personal level and finds him likable because they want to believe that such a great success may be in their own future. He's become a champion of the "average Joe."

By now you've most likely realized that you don't have to find something supernatural about yourself and your company to capitalize on. What you must do is find out how to use the special traits that you already have.

Analyze the obvious

Start by identifying what it is about you and your business that may be of special interest to others and, therefore, the media. Target three or four areas that have genuine possibilities.

1. What business are you in?

2. What are your specific products or services?

3. Who are your customers?

4. What market do you target? Is your product or service used by teenagers? Older women? Business executives?

5. What geographical area do you dominate or want to penetrate?

6. Who are your competitors?

7. Why do people do business with you?

Once you've answered these questions, review the information carefully to find out if there are specific characteristics that make you unusual or have the potential to differentiate you and your company from others. You may find yourself adding more detail. As an example:

1. What business are you in?

Short answer: Management consultant.

More detail: Assisting businesses in maximizing the dynamics of diversity.

2. What is your product or service?

Short answer: Training and development programs.

More detail: Creating and implementing half-day and full-day programs designed to improve employee performance and teamwork within a diverse work force.

3. Who are your customers?

Short answer: Construction companies.

More detail: Small and mid-size construction companies that have mandated diversity in their work force as a result of government contracts.

Consider carefully the seventh question: Why do people do business with you? You must understand that this question is the key to a good PR campaign as well as any follow-up marketing efforts. Your ultimate goal is to find more customers, so knowing why your current customers have made your business their choice will offer key information on what to promote.

Remembering that you don't always see yourself as others see you should lead you to the next step in this exercise. Ask the same series of questions of your employees (if you have any), your business associates, and for an interesting perspective, your customers or clients. Find out what aspects of your business have made the strongest and the most favorable impressions on them.

If you find that these answers are very different from your own, step back and give that some serious consideration. Perhaps they see your business, product, or service as having a value far different than your original conception. Or you may be giving mixed messages because of the name of your company, the way you advertise or market, or you may be exceeding even your own expectations by the way you serve accounts. By now you should be getting a clear image of the public perception of your business.

As you gather this information, what may surface are interesting and unique characteristics of your business that had never occurred to you. At the conclusion of this exercise, you should, however, be able to identify some specific aspects about yourself and your business that you may be able to parlay into media exposure.

Examples:

- ♦ I am one of the few women to own and operate a barber shop.
- ♦ My restaurant is the only one in Fairbanks, Alaska, to specialize in great Southern-style barbecue.
- ♦ We have a very public-spirited work force and we do extraordinary service in the community, such as building homes with Habitat for Humanity.
- ♦ Our place of business is in an unusual location—an historic refurbished church.
- ♦ I am a noted expert in my field—the author of a book and syndicated newspaper column.

Consider the story of one auto repair shop and how it took its uniqueness to achieve strong success: Lucille Treganowan was a divorced mother of four, working as the bookkeeper in a transmission repair business. In her desire to become proficient at her own job, Lucille began to learn more about the actual transmission repair—the names and use of parts in a transmission and the cost and price of services. Eventually, she felt confident that she could run her own shop. After becoming convinced that her future was stymied where she was, Lucille went into business for herself.

In the mid-1970s there were very few women involved in the auto repair business so this was a natural area for PR. Would men (who made the majority of repair arrangements) trust their car repair to a woman?

Lucille didn't hide the fact that the company was owned and operated by a woman—after all, it was called "Transmissions by Lucille." But she didn't actively promote the fact, either. Very soon, she learned that her customers chose her business *because* it was run by a woman. They told her that they saw a woman mechanic as more trustworthy and felt that their car would be cleaner after the repair. Lucille takes care to make sure expectations are met.

Given the green light to promote her gender, Lucille proceeded full-speed ahead and, over the years, has developed a successful business. Her second location has beautiful flower pots in front of it. Although her business remains local in Pennsylvania, she has become a bit of a national phenomenon with a book and TV show both entitled *Lucille's Car Care Clinic*. Lucille's Tutu is definitely pink!

Making a gray tutu interesting

After doing an in-depth review of his business, a management consultant still could not find the area that was unique enough to promote to the public. So he went to his customers to ask for their input. At first, it seemed as if they were just reiterating the facts he had already considered—but with one exception. The team-building exercises were repeatedly described as "fun" and "energizing." In fact, all respondents said they enjoyed the seminars; many said their outside life had benefited, and a few even claimed that they would have attended even if the company hadn't sponsored the program.

It occurred to the consultant that the programs he designed had real benefit to average people within the community. By sponsoring a number of free seminars to benefit nonprofit and community agencies, he could be of value and perhaps get "media" coverage as well. The results were terrific! The attendees appreciated the opportunity and a local TV station gave coverage. The local minority press wrote an in-depth article. His business definitely benefited.

So you see, it doesn't matter if you are a female mechanic, a community-spirited consultant, or a mild-mannered "average Joe." There is something special about you and your company that is interesting enough to promote. The payoff is excellent—free publicity for your effort. Go over every step in this chapter and you should be able to discover the color of *your* tutu—the unique personality of your business.

If you are still scratching your head after some serious consideration, then you may be a candidate for a professional *tutu expert*— a PR consultant. In later chapters we will give you more guidelines for making this decision.

Chapter 4

Now appearing in the center ring...

Communicating Effectively With the Media

Your task in the previous chapter was to identify the color of your tutu—in other words, become familiar with what makes you stand out from the crowd. The next step is to work on ways to tell your story to the media and, ultimately, to the public. *How* you tell your story may well be as important as what the story is about.

It is likely that if you are in the early stages of a bootstrap public relations campaign, the role of spokesperson will be yours. Therefore, you must learn what it takes to communicate effectively through the media.

Later on, as your business grows and becomes more profitable and your message is targeted to a larger audience, you may want to consider hiring a "talking head," someone who will serve as your liaison to the press. Here, the trained media spokesperson knows exactly how to present your message to the public so it will be given the widest and most favorable coverage.

But for now, this job will likely fall to you. And you will discover that you can learn to handle yourself quite well if you take the time to think of the needs of your audience.

Take aim and shoot for PAR

In this case PAR stands for *presence, articulation,* and being *real.* These are the three key attributes of a successful spokesperson. You should carefully consider your own skills in each area and be prepared to work to develop your own strong style.

1. Presence. Presence is almost an undefinable quality yet one that virtually everyone recognizes when they see it. Television is the media for which presence is most critical. However, a strong presence can be sensed in a good print or radio interview, as well.

A very wide variety of individuals have an appealing presence and it has nothing to do with sex, age, or even physical appearance. Oprah has it and so does Rosie O'Donnell. Everyone could feel the energy in the presence of Tiger Woods from the first time he appeared in public. George Burns kept it until he was close to 100, and "it" was evident in Michael Jackson when he was only 5. But you don't have to be a star to develop presence. Many people have the potential to transmit a strong presence.

Perhaps presence may best be described as a strong sense of self, enhanced by a healthy dose of confidence. Most entrepreneurs already possess the ingredients for positive presence—it is a necessary component in creating and promoting a new business venture. You probably just need some tips on how to enhance your presence, and some practice under actual interview circumstances.

2. Articulation. In a world of 30-second sound bites, the ability to articulate your position quickly and clearly is critical. When you're on the air or your quote appears in print, it is imperative that you capture the attention of your audience by using strong words, concise statements, and a substantial amount of enthusiasm.

Your words and the way you say them must be effective enough to get the attention of the audience. You want your key points to be remembered, and that requires a real skill in communication. The good news here is that this skill can be taught, and practice almost always improves the performance. If you want to measure your own current ability to articulate effectively, ask yourself the following questions:

1. Am I usually concise and to the point or do I tend to drone on?

2. Do I have any bad habits that can annoy my listener, such as clicking my tongue, taking long pauses, or saying "um," or "you know"?

3. Do I use words that are easily understood (*The New York Times* writes at an eighth-grade level) or do I use a technical or clinical vocabulary?

4. Do I have a strong regional accent or have a tendency to use slang? (As a rule, this doesn't fly well on the national level.)

5. Can I field tough questions without getting angry or sounding defensive?

6. Do I tend to make too many "off-the-cuff" comments that may be misinterpreted?

7. Can I be relaxed when I am asked a question that I don't understand or haven't any good response for? Do I try to fast-talk my way through a bad answer?

The answers to these questions should give you a good indication of how articulate and prepared you are to "go public." Your ability to be articulate may have a real impact on the future of your company. Evaluate your answers and concentrate on those areas in which you need improvement.

3. Being real. The definition listed under the word "real" is "not artificial, fraudulent, illusory, or apparent." You may have a presence—and yet not be real. For example, basketball star Dennis Rodman has a larger-than-life presence but few would describe him as someone who seems real. Oprah Winfrey and Rosie O'Donnell have a substantial dose of both and this is the basis for their drawing power. They reveal their passions, share their fears, and openly discuss their hopes and disappointments. The audience gets the impression that underneath it all, they are "just like you and me."

At this point you may be saying to yourself, "This is easy, I am real!" Or you may be saying, "I'm not a media star." As a matter of fact, you may get nervous just thinking about appearing on radio or television—so how could anyone think that you are anything *but* real? Often when we are unprepared and undertrained for public appearances, we overcompensate by trying to seem too confident or in control. The result? You won't come off as real.

If you have made public appearances in the past, have one coming up in the near future, or can schedule something to try out your style, you can make an analysis of how you come off to your audience. Review an old tape if you can get one (perhaps you will have the chance to ask the radio or TV producer for a tape of any performance). Or bring a friend to an upcoming event. Then ask yourself the following questions about how the audience reacts to you— *not* about how you felt while being interviewed. These are tools to help you evaluate your performance.

1. Do you make direct eye contact with the person speaking to you?

2. Do you smile naturally, or do your smiles seem forced?

3. Does your overall approach and attitude appear upbeat and optimistic?

4. Do you have a sense of humor and willingness to laugh at yourself?

5. Do you communicate with facial and body language that are in synch with your thoughts and words?

6. Do you appear approachable and accessible?

Test your performance against what is PAR for this course, *presence, articulation* and being *real*. Remember, the more experience you get, the more you will learn and the better your image will transmit. If you are not comfortable with how you appear or if you feel that you need to make progress at a faster rate, you can find a professional to coach you in all the right moves.

Hide your weaknesses—hire a media trainer

Fear of public speaking grips a large percentage of the population. Even those who do it regularly will report that they get nervous and sometimes experience doubt about their effectiveness. Working on your technique will help to assure you that the message you intend to send is indeed the message that your listeners, viewers, and readers receive. Professionals known as media trainers can coach you to be natural, at ease, and effective when being interviewed. Often they have had on-air experience as reporters or show hosts; many media trainers are also public relations consultants.

Normally your session (or sessions) will be taped and you can use the copies to continue to practice. The hourly charge may be high ($50 to $250 per hour) but you may need as few as one or two sessions to put you on the right track. A media trainer will likely cover the following areas:

♦ How to control butterflies and performance anxiety.

♦ How to project your voice.

♦ Correcting improper speech patterns.

♦ Choosing language that is easily understood.

♦ How to project a sense of confidence as well as passion about your topic.

♦ Wardrobe choices that are flattering.

♦ Understanding your own body language and learning how to use it to your advantage.

Your local business directories will likely have listings for media trainers and image consultants (individuals who specialize on the last two items listed). You also might consider joining the local chapter of the National Speakers Association. (Look in your phone book or call the national headquarters at 602-968-2552 for a referral.) If you are interested in ongoing speaking and communications practice, look into joining a local chapter of Toastmasters International (the national number is 714-858-8255). At Toastmasters, you will give both long and short talks, and your fellow members will give you constructive feedback about your effectiveness. Although your learning process will take more time with an organization than with the individual attention of a media trainer, the cost will be substantially lower. And within a number of organizations, you may be able to get video- and audio-assisted training and perform mock media interviews as part of your membership fee.

With awareness and practice, you can emerge as a dynamic and captivating spokesperson, exuding warmth, wisdom, and wit.

Chapter 5

Do I need a tutu expert?

Before You Hire a PR Agency

A good public relations campaign can become a key element in the continuing success of your business. If you have the time and the determination to do it yourself, you can make good publicity happen because it is *your* story and *your* passion that you are pitching. And the cost can be very minimal. Needless to say, the expenditure will increase dramatically if and when you decide to hire outside help. But there are times when this should be considered and when that decision is made, you must find the best PR agency—or "tutu expert"—and learn how to manage the costs, as well.

Even if the funds are available, this should not be the sole determining factor in your decision. Instead, ask yourself a few questions to see if it makes sense to hire a PR agency.

1. Is your schedule so full that you barely have 15 minutes to relax and eat lunch? Are you sure that there is no way to restructure your schedule to run any sort of meaningful campaign?

2. Are you paralyzed with fear just thinking about doing publicity and know that you'll never stop procrastinating?

3. Do you need to reach a national audience or a very specialized, sophisticated area of the media?

4. Is your business in crisis and you're up to your eyeballs in challenges? Is the media sniffing around already and you feel that you must get out your own spin on the story now?

5. Are you planning a one-time big event that needs all the intensive effort you can muster?

If you answered yes to any of these questions and the funds are available, you might want to consider finding your own PR expert. Remember, you may be able to find someone to work with you to show you the ropes and help you plan and conduct the public relations campaign yourself and keep the cost in check. You never know unless you ask.

Where do you find a good PR expert?

The best reference for any outside consultant is the personal recommendation of a business associate, so start by asking around within your community. Next, you might ask a member of the local media for recommendations. If you don't find any good contacts from that effort, you might consider this: Follow a great public relations campaign back to its origins (the company or individual who is being featured) and ask them which public relations firm is responsible for their success. Most business owners will be flattered by your contact and, if they aren't direct competitors, they probably wouldn't mind giving you that information.

If you can't find a good candidate through personal research, try looking in the national directories, *O'Dwyers Directory of Public Relations* and *Public Relations Society of America* (both are listed in the resource section of this book). There is a listing under public relations, as well, in your local business phone directory.

Be sure to remember that before you engage someone you don't know, it is critical to check references—and dig even deeper when possible. When you talk to references given by the firm you're considering, ask if they know anybody else who has worked with the professional you are considering. Check the new names out as well.

How much does it cost?

As with any outside consultant, it is important to understand how you will be charged and to mutually determine an estimated budget for your work. Don't be afraid to ask questions. The following are general parameters for public relations fees.

1. **Hourly.** Based on your area of the country and the experience of your expert, the hourly fees may be as low as $25 and as high as $200. And within a project, there may be lower fees for research time and higher fees for in-person time from the same expert. And if you are using someone from any distance, there could be travel time as well as out-of-pocket expenses.

    The time your PR expert spends with you will not be the only hours he or she charges you for. Working on your behalf behind the scenes, doing research, developing strategies, cultivating leads, and media follow-ups are all billable time to you. Keep in mind, there are some experts who work on the phone, fax, and Internet and almost never meet clients in person.

    Always set a maximum amount of hours in any billing cycle and get these agreements in writing. No one can know absolutely how much progress you will make in a set number of hours (it may be faster as well as slower)— it's good policy to create general guidelines.

2. **Retainer Basis.** If your needs are more general and ongoing, the answer may be a monthly retainer arrangement that includes up to a set number of hours each month to develop all the public relations opportunities your expert can uncover. You wouldn't want your expert to stop just short of a goal, so there may be an overage agreement that allows for extra hours to be billed in excess.

   The retainer is determined by the number of hours times the hourly rate (for example, 12 hours a month at $100 an hour would be a $1,200 monthly retainer). The more hours you commit to, the greater the possibility that your hourly rate will be discounted a bit. It's certainly worth some negotiation.

3. **Package Price.** If you have a single special event or short-term critical period in which to promote something, the arrangement that may best suit this purpose is one price to complete the job from planning to implementation. Full discussion and understanding is, of course, of utmost importance in this type of deal. Make sure you establish the specific goal and charge so you aren't surprised with a bill for extras.

4. **Percentage of Outcome.** This is the trickiest of all arrangements and simply should never be tried by a business new to the world of public relations. Good public relations will virtually always create greater interest and better sales, but attaching one to the other is often more art than science. Perhaps if you are having a single large sale event, you can set aside a percentage to pay for public relations, but it will be difficult to attribute an exact portion of the revenue generated by the media effort.

Remember that for all of the pricing strategies, there will likely be extra costs that aren't anticipated. You will be charged all out-of-pocket expenses, such as phone calls, printing costs, and postage. Some of these costs, in fact, may be marked up above their actual costs. Ask about the policy on this and, as in other cases, establish maximum dollars to be spent.

Before you hire, ask questions

The best-case scenario would be that you will have more than one expert candidate and that you will be able to make an informed choice after meeting with them. But even if you only have one, be sure to conduct an exploratory interview to make sure that you have a good match.

Following are some of the areas you want to cover:

1. Ask to see sample media kits that your candidate has created. You can get a sense of the promotional style—glitzy or conservative or in-between—and determine if this is compatible with how you see yourself. Don't judge by only one sample—try to see three or more.

2. After discussing your goals, ask your candidate to give you an overview of how he or she would go about achieving them. You want to find out as early as possible if your expert can accomplish your work in what seems a reasonable time frame. If he or she is used to working with larger companies and larger budgets, it may be difficult to get you where you need to be within your time frame and budget. If you are new, small, or on a tight budget, make sure you hire someone who understands this reality.

3. What sort of local (and national, if appropriate) media contacts does the individual or agency have? The better the existing relationships, the more effective a campaign you will get for your money. Newer practitioners may still be in the mode of establishing these connections, and it may take longer to get your company placements.

4. Does the expert or agency have any ideas about positioning you and your business for the media? The two things you will find out here is whether your candidate knows something about you already and how creative he or she is. You must realize that it will take some time to really find the hook for your business, but you need to see something at the start.

5. How does the candidate charge? By the hour? How much? Is there a difference in research and face time (in person)? Any mark-up on outside services? How often are bills sent? Ask any and all questions you can think of along these lines and measure the answers you get as an important criteria of your decision. Be sure you feel your candidate is being straightforward.

6. As you interview candidates, whether in person or over the phone, listen carefully to how they sound. Look for good phone voice. Most good public relations happens on the phone, so your expert should sound friendly and confident and be easy to listen to.

There may be other questions and other areas you want to explore. If this is the case, please do so. The working relationship between you and your public relations person is critical to the success of the work. Your expert will be creating relationships between you and members of the media that you hope will remain in place for years—take the time and make the best possible decision.

How to evaluate the work of a PR expert

The amount of value that you can attribute to a concerted public relations campaign is somewhat difficult to assess, because there will be short-term gain and long-term gain. Over the short-term, you may be able to value the air time or page space as the cost of advertising and put an actual number to the placements.

As an example:

Local print media

Paper	Circulation	Placement	Ad Cost
Business News	26,000	1 page photo 1 page copy	$10,100
Local Daily	250,000	Cover of Business Section	$15,000
Regional Paper	6,000	Cover Story	$2,500
		Total Local Media	$27,600

National Press

Magazine	Circulation	Placement	Ad Cost
#1	18,000	1 full page	$3,500
#2	22,000	1 full page	$2,300
#3	23,000	3 pages/color	$13,100
#4	90,000	3 pages/color	$14,500
		Total National Media	$33,400
GRAND TOTAL			$61,000

This example is based on a real campaign run for a commercial photographer over a period of two-and-a-half years. Over that time, he paid a media consultant about $20,000 in fees. At first glance, it might be seen that he received two-and-a-half times the value spent.

This may not represent the entire story. Over a period of time, these new relationships may bring important ongoing coverage.

The next questions to ask involve the effect of the campaign on the revenues and profits of the company. Did the increased exposure bring new customers in the door? Did it result in increased sales? Did the exposure bring more sophisticated (or different in any positive way) customers to the business? Did their purchases result in higher profits? This may be the best outcome because newer customers may purchase in beneficial ways, such as higher volume per transaction, which lowers costs and raises the bottom line. Good public relations is about building credibility and interest—and that results in attracting a solid customer base.

In many instances, public relations coverage is more valuable than advertising: Anyone can buy ad space, but the perception is that only the special companies get news coverage.

Finally, when determining the value of your public relations expert, remember that the media contacts you make will continue, particularly if you have learned from your expert how to keep them active. In addition, many of the articles that have appeared will remain in the research files and will be referred to in the future.

Chapter 6

Getting ready for the highwire act

Planning Your PR Campaign

Whether you decide to do your public relations campaign on your own or hire a PR expert, the first step to making good publicity happen is to *create a plan*. This is an exercise that you cannot skip—it will allow you to determine whether to narrow your scope or broaden your horizons by identifying the steps to reaching your goal. You must allow sufficient time to develop and implement a successful strategy. We will cover three separate phases over the next three chapters; they are as follows:

1. Develop and write a plan including targeting specific media.
2. Create, package, and distribute to the media.
3. Follow up and implement action.

Begin by brainstorming

Don't be limited by the traditional perceptions of public relations—use your imagination and decide what will work uniquely well for your company. In the process, there are a number of issues you should think through because they are the key elements of creating a successful plan.

♦ What is my focus—how will I use it to attract the attention I seek?

♦ Is my campaign for one story (perhaps covered in several places), or am I looking to develop contacts for a series of stories?

♦ Is my campaign local? Regional? National? International?

♦ What is my time frame?

♦ Does my business (or the event I'm promoting) require visual support (TV or print coverage with photos) or can the story be told in words alone?

♦ We will be successful if we accomplish our goal to

_____.

[Fill this in with specific goals such as: build a stronger public image, increase inquiries, shoot for higher sales, concentrate on higher profits. If you don't know what you want, you're unlikely to be successful in your efforts.]

First step: Find your target media

Now that your strategy for gaining publicity is beginning to take shape, you're going to be putting it into a plan that you can then use as a road map to take you where you want to go. A major element of that plan is identifying your targeted media outlets and including specific information about who they are and how to reach them. Start with the print media—there are more of them and they tend to have more time and space to develop business stories.

1. Begin by listing local daily, weekly, and monthly publications.

2. Identify any local monthly magazines.

3. List local and regional radio stations (be sure you understand the format of each).

4. Check out local cable TV stations.

5. Look into local network TV affiliates.

Enlarge your list with:

6. Statewide print media (newspapers and magazines in other cities of your region, including close-by states).

7. An expanded electronic media list of radio and TV stations.

8. Trade (or professional) association newsletters.

9. Alumni newsletters or magazines.

10. Your hometown media (if you are originally from another place).

If you have a story with national appeal:

11. Specialized monthly magazines may be interested in a story that has application to its readers, such as a general business tip applicable to many professional publications.

12. General-interest weekly and monthly publications such as *People* or *Time* or *The New Yorker* are often searching for human interest stories.

13. The national newspapers such as *USA Today* or *The Wall Street Journal* are harder to penetrate even with a great story, although you may find a local contact. (Here is one place a PR expert may really be important.)

14. There are specialized national cable networks that may be appropriate.

15. The big fish are NBC, ABC, CBS, FOX, and CNN—how about a segment on the *Today Show*?

You will need to compile a complete list of all of the possible media sources you might contact. Your list should include as much up-to-date information as you can find. Make sure that your list is relevant to your story. For example, you would not send a business story to an entertainment magazine. Remember to check for accuracy. This can be accomplished by a phone call and is definitely worth the effort.

The following is information that makes up the basics of a media list:

1. **Name of media source.** Be sure to include such detail as call letters for electronic media, whether the source is local, regional, or national, its circulation or market reach, and reader/listener/viewer profile.

2. **Contact person.** You may have several contacts at a single outlet. In print, it may be the name of the feature editor, the metro editor, the business editor or specific reporters. In electronic, the contact may be the producer, assignment editor, or an on-air personality who books his or her own show, or even a reporter who looks for good stories to develop. Some magazines have regular contributing freelance writers who develop stories independently. Each contact name should have a separate listing.

3. **Contact information.** This, of course, will include address and phone number. But don't forget, in an industry in which your contacts may rarely sit down to answer their phones, fax numbers and e-mail addresses increase your ability to stay in touch. Also, make sure you jot down any Web site addresses attached to your media sources.

4. **Notes.** The general focus of the media outlet should be a part of the notes, as well as areas of specific interest such as a column on small business news or emphasis on particular neighborhoods. Lead times and deadline dates should be a part of your notes. Sending an announcement about a June event two weeks after the June issue closes won't get you anywhere. Special holiday editions, annual reports, and single-focus editions should be listed in your notes.

5. **Previous placements.** Once you have become active in promoting your business to the media, you'll want to track the mentions you have receive. A week after one good article is too soon to pitch for a new one. Keep a record of placement history for each media source. Should you want to get reprints of any article (or a tape of a show), knowing the exact date (and time) will come in handy to expedite your request.

Your contact list can be kept on large note cards, which you file alphabetically—or on a sophisticated database. The latter will be easier but they both will work. If you are really serious about this, you can pick up specific software that will allow you to print labels and track calls, as well as broadcast fax and e-mail through your modem.

Make sure you guard your list closely (always keep a backup) and update it on a regular basis. A good list is worth gold. Without one, you'll struggle with your publicity campaign.

Write your plan

Any good strategy improves when it is written down. A written plan allows you to see the strengths and weaknesses, identify specific goals, and set timelines for completion. You will be able to evaluate the feasibility of your plan and establish benchmarks by which to measure your progress.

The basic elements of your plan will be the following:

1. Goals. You must create reasonable goals in any plan, but particularly if you are attempting publicity for the first time. Unless your story is very unusual or the timing is absolutely perfect, the coverage on the first go-around may be limited. But remember, one of the beneficial outcomes is that you are developing media relationships that will make subsequent campaigns more effective.

It's important to make your goals as specific and quantifiable as you can. Perhaps your story is about a special, one-day holiday event your community center is sponsoring. Included on your list of goals might be to be featured in at least three of the four holiday issues of your area's print publications, and to be listed in the community calendars in every newspaper and magazine. You might also set a goal of landing feature spots with at least two of the four local news shows.

2. Media list. You may be creating your media list specifically for this campaign, in which case your entire list will be in play. Later on, you will want to review your database and choose only those media outlets that are appropriate for the specific story you are pitching. Based on the example given in the previous discussion of goals, you would include on your media list all of the publications in your area that have special holiday issues and community calendars. You would also include local radio and TV news shows. It is possible that you might add the local business newspaper. If you believe there is something especially unique about your community center's holiday event—say, a nationally known celebrity will be making an appearance—you might add some regional or national media sources, as well.

3. Required resources. Two types of resources will be required to implement your publicity plan: First, you will need to develop printed (or taped) material that you will send to the media. Don't forget to set a budget for the production of this material.

Second, you will need human resources, which will be needed to complete all of the steps you are identifying as a part of this plan. You will learn as you read on in this section that just sending your material won't achieve the results you desire. One of the most critical elements to your success will be the follow-up once your package has been distributed. As you develop this phase of your plan, you may realize that the time-sensitive demands are more than you are equipped to handle. This should have been a part of your decision-making process about hiring a PR expert and you may now see the need to utilize one on a part-time basis. You are trying to balance the available financial resources and this can be a major project cost.

If you are attempting to do this alone, you may not have the time to make all of your follow-up calls in a timely manner. And what is your availability to answer questions, schedule interviews, and make all other necessary arrangements? Keeping costs down is good, but getting the work done is critical. Don't lose opportunities because you are shorthanded. Hire the help you need!

4. Timeline. Using the information you have already gathered, the real meat and potatoes of a publicity plan is in the timeline you establish and how disciplined you are in living up to it. Begin with step one and set specific dates for the completion of each required task. A sample plan may be structured like the one on page 62.

5. Establish outcome criteria. The final phase of your campaign will be the determination of your success in reaching your goals. Did you receive good coverage? Increased customer interest? Increased sales?

This evaluation will assist you in planning and conducting future public relations campaigns and may help you to decide if you need expert help on the next go-around. Keep your expectations realistic and your evaluation very candid.

Timeline

Goal: To conduct a publicity campaign from (time frame) to achieve greater public awareness about (specific aspect) of my profession or business.

Steps to Reach That Goal:

By _____

(date),

I will have identified the key focus of my publicity campaign.

By _____

(date),

I will have targeted the specific media outlets I will pursue.

By _____

(date),

I will have created the media kit, press release or other written material I will need.

By _____

(date),

I will have completed distribution of my material to targeted media.

By _____

(date),

I will begin my follow-up with media and continue until (date), the end of this phase.

By _____

(date),

I will evaluate my progress and determine my future publicity strategy.

Chapter 7

How to get an elephant in an envelope

Creating Your Media Kit

If you saw an elephant walking down the street, you might realize something unusual was going on—but you would know little more than that. Even if you were a reporter, you'd probably need to gather more information before you turned your story in. Where did the elephant come from—the circus or the zoo? How did the elephant escape? Are there other elephants that may follow suit? Has this happened before? Is it an African elephant or an Indian elephant? Although the headline and key focus of the story may be "Dumbo Takes Elephant Walk," it will take some background information to flesh out the story and put it into context.

The same goes for your story: Don't assume the media will know all about you—you've got to supply them with the background information that may not be part of the main focus of your publicity. This information might include the background of your business—when and how you got started, what other types of business or services you provide, who your clients are, and more. Providing all this detail may require several sheets of paper, perhaps a brochure or two, maybe even photographs. When you gather all this material together along with your "story," you create a package called a "media kit."

Not every business or professional needs to go to the time and expense of creating a media kit (also referred to as a press kit). But, then, a media kit does not have to be an elaborate, high-cost, printed work. What you are looking for is a collection of materials that will help the reporter do a better job in reporting your story. There are a number of items that will be included beyond your news release, and they all should be packaged in a nice folder or binder. Read on to learn about all of the aspects and implications of a media kit and then decide whether or not you really need one.

When do you need a media kit?

If your story is simple—the announcement of a new location, a new product, or an important personnel change—a one-page press release may cover it. But when you are making the effort to develop comprehensive coverage, a media kit may be critical, particularly in the following situations:

1. At a press conference. Needless to say, if you have reached the point that you have called a press conference, you are at a point where the media kit is necessary. Your media kit should provide all of the background information a reporter will need to write the story. Knowing that this material is in hand allows the reporter time to focus on the spokesperson and the reason for the conference.

2. At a special event. A media kit may serve several purposes if you are planning a special event. First, a very appealing kit may heighten the likelihood that a reporter will attend your event. Second, the background data included may mean that you get more in-depth coverage because the information will be readily available while the story is being written.

3. When a press release simply can't cover it all. Perhaps you are planning to launch a new product or open up your business at a new location. A news release may give the required information about the latest addition to your business, but there is still a great deal of background about you, your company history, and past success that would be valuable to include. A 15-page press release might turn off a reporter but a well-presented media kit will create interest.

What are the elements of a great media kit?

There are a number of items that might be contained in any media kit and yours may have all or just a few. The quantity of items is far less important than the quality. Beyond the press release, you should include whatever information is relevant. What follows are the basic components you will want to include:

Press release

This critical piece of information should contain all of the essential facts (who, what, where, when, and why) and tell the complete story as concisely as possible. If you are promoting a special event, list the schedule with specific time slots (Mayor to speak at 3 p.m., etc.) so media can decide when to attend. A well-written release typically becomes the basis for a story.

Fact sheet

Also called a *stat sheet*, this contains data only, without any spin or persuasive language. Formatted as a one-sheet piece, each main fact is emphasized in a bulleted format—easy to find and easy to read. For example, if you are announcing a new location, be sure to include the new address, phone number, hours of operation, key personnel, and any unique features of that particular location.

Backgrounder

All of the basic information about you and your company is contained including history, descriptions of principals, areas of influence, accomplishments and awards, industry statistics, and perhaps mention of top clients.

This need not be on a single page. In fact, if there is enough to say, you may include one full page on each topic.

You may also write the backgrounder in a question-and-answer format. You will be able to answer what you believe are the most frequently asked questions about the nature, quality, and value of your service or products. If used, this would be a great advertising vehicle.

Reprints of articles

If you have written—or have been featured or interviewed in—articles published in newspapers or magazines, include clear copies in your media kit. If the list is quite long, include the best articles and a log of other interviews in print, radio, or TV. Be sure to include the name of show, host, and air date.

Quote sheet

If you have received great quotes from notable people in the community or industry, recap these testimonials on one sheet. Include titles of the people quoted and ask their permission. If any are willing to be interviewed further, add this feature and a phone number, as well.

Biographies

Not a resume, a media biography is an easy-to-read introduction that should feature what is interesting and important about your work and accomplishments if you are a feature of the story. If you're having a special event with a prominent person, a biography for this individual should be included, as well. It can be a few sentences to a few paragraphs.

Photos

Include photos pertinent to your story. This might include "head" shots—above-the-shoulders pictures—of the principals of your company, product shots, candid photos of customers using your product or service, or pictures directly related to the event or topic of your story. Often, print media are limited to black-and-white shots, although more publications—even newspapers—feature artwork in color. Be sure to attach a caption to every photo, identifying key people and how to attribute the photo. (If you had a professional photographer take the shots, you will most likely be required to tell the publication to include a "credit line.") Photos can be a very important component of your media kit—many publications base their decision to cover a story on whether they have good art to accompany the text.

Clip sheet

Also referred to as a sidebar or canned piece, this is a finished story, camera-ready with artwork in place. Great for smaller publications that have staffing restraints—they can use this as a fill-in or as a sidebar to run with your feature article. An example? Let's say you're promoting your new pet bed-and-breakfast. A side story about the champion Pekingese who stayed at your lodge and then went on to win the dog show the next day might make a great "human" interest story.

Brochures

Your sales brochure, operating manual, or annual report can be included, particularly if they relate to the article being pitched. In most cases, these pieces offer quite a bit of "background" information and perhaps some historical perspective. Often, your brochure will feature photos or descriptions or even testimonials. Even though the reporter will realize these materials are sales-oriented, they will offer valuable insight and allow the individual to develop a clearer picture of your product, your service, or your company.

Gimmicks

If a gimmick really fits with your promotion, use it. You want your media kit to stand out from all of the other material received. How about small elephants in pink tutus on keychains to promote this book? Food products are usually a hit—make sure they travel well. Also, items that will be used—or seen—frequently by the recipient are winners. Refrigerator magnets, key chains, calendars, and pens get a lot of exposure. Use your imagination! But make sure the item is relevant to your pitch. After all, such gimmicks typically cost a little more than the paper mailing.

What is an electronic media kit?

For greater impact, particularly to show how visual your story is or how good a spokesperson you are, you can create a videotape presentation, often referred to as an EMK (electronic media kit) or EPK (electronic press kit). Your video can be designed as a clip reel with several segments showcasing more than one aspect of your story, or it may be one continuous piece. The length should be 6 to 8 minutes and the tape should be professional quality on ¾" or 1" tape.

Don't send out an unsolicited EMK. Begin with a traditional media kit and mention that an electronic version is available. If an editor or producer is interested, he or she will let you know.

The media kit design

A fancy kit is not a necessity—use a decent folder and organize your material well so that everything is easy to find and easy to read. The most popular format is a pocket folder: It may be printed, embossed, or plain with a neat, easy-to-read label on the front containing identifying information.

Put background information in the left pocket and current data/most important data in the right pocket (it's the side that will be seen first). The stand-alone news release should be on top in the right pocket—or attach it to the cover of the package.

You may also use a three-ring binder or spiral-bind the information with tabs. If money isn't an object, a "stepped" format is effective. Each page is of decreasing height, which makes the pages stand out. A similar effect may be achieved by color-coding the related information (white news release, background information in pastel yellow, fact sheet in green). Don't use dark colors—they don't copy well.

Keep the look consistent with the story—don't package serious information in a cute cover. And always print extras to use as a sales tool at business meetings, conferences, and trade shows.

If you use the services of a graphic designer for your logo, letterhead, business card, brochures, and other materials, you might consider having a standard media kit package designed as well. This way, you'll know that the "look" of this important piece will complement and match your other materials. Although hiring an outside designer to create these pieces can be expensive, if you invest in a good design, it may carry you through many promotions.

How do I send out my media kit?

The easiest and most economical way to get your media kit out is to send it via regular mail. The problem with this? You'll never know if it has reached its destination unless you call. You could use an overnight service that requires a signature for receipt.

You can drop off the kit personally but don't expect to be able to hand it directly to the editor, producer, or reporter. You will most likely be asked to leave it at the reception desk and assume it will get to the right hands. This is why it is so important that you have developed a media kit that stands out from the crowd. Most likely, your media kit will pass through many hands—a receptionist, an assistant, perhaps an intern—before it reaches the person you intended it for.

Media kit effectiveness

If you want your kit to be well-received, you should show that you have carefully considered all the elements and style that make for a standout package. Your extra effort may keep your media kit out of the slush pile.

- ◆ Colored paper is okay—not too dark and, remember, neon is hard on the eyes.
- ◆ *Never* misspell anything—check for accuracy.
- ◆ Send what's useful—don't try to pitch two unrelated stories at the same time.
- ◆ Names, addresses, and phone numbers of the contact person should be on every piece of material.

♦ Type information double-spaced on one side of the paper.

♦ Don't try to be too cute or too clever. Facts sell themselves—don't kill them with gimmicks.

♦ Don't tape the kit to death. Make sure it's easy to open.

♦ Be sensitive to media deadlines and submission dates. If you want an article to be in a specific issue, the deadline may be several months earlier. If your information is *really* time-sensitive, put on the outside envelope "Dated Material—Please Open Immediately." Again, *only* put this message on dated material.

♦ Personalize your media kit to the appropriate person. A call in advance to get the correct name is a worthwhile effort.

♦ Media kits are not returned—don't call to get yours back. It's in your interest if it is kept on file even if it won't be used at the present time.

Chapter 8

Encore! Encore!

Follow-up: A Crucial Step in Your PR Plan

Once your promotion has been packaged in a kit and sent to its media destination, the next step is yours, as well. You must follow up with a phone call to make sure your materials have been received, answer any questions and seal the deal. Getting up the nerve to make a 30-second phone call could make the difference between living in obscurity on a pile on an editor's desk and gaining fame and fortune. Think of the process as a courtship. Expect to get a date!

Before you pick up the phone

If you did your job well in putting together an attention-getting press release and a helpful media kit, you shouldn't have a difficult time making your follow-up calls. All you have to do is refer to that great lead line in your press release or some unforgettable element of your press kit to trigger the memory of your media source. If you are still feeling a bit reticent about getting on the phone and following up with the members of the media who have received your material, remember the following:

- ◆ Reporters need sources. You're offering material for them to build a story to fill air time or page space. Most editors and producers respect this fact and will welcome your call.

♦ The call will show how much you really care about your
  story.

♦ You will learn about the specific needs of the station or
  publication and you may be able to assist in finding an
  angle for your story.

♦ Even if you can't get a placement now, you might be
  planting the seeds for a future relationship. The second
  call later on down the road will be easier than the first—
  you may even make a new friend.

♦ Scoring a win with the media may offer unexpected
  surprises. The story you get placed may lead to other
  publicity opportunities. The next time, the media may be
  courting you!

The worst time to call

When on deadline, staff at publications or broadcast media are
under a lot of pressure and the stress level gets very high. You don't
want to get off on the wrong foot, so do your homework. When
dealing with print media, call ahead and find out the deadline dates
(or time of day, if you're dealing with a daily)—and avoid making
your follow-up calls during these times. After all, you know how
you feel when you're trying to get out of the house and the phone
rings.

Right before a show goes on the air, radio, or television, everyone has their focus on that day's production—not the future. For a
daily show, wait at least a half-hour after the show goes off the air.
For a weekly show, call the day after.

If you inadvertently call at a bad time, back off as soon as you
discover this (the irritated tone or abrupt responses of your media

source will be an indication). Express understanding of the pressure your contact is under, and offer to call back at a better time.

Preparing for the call

Like a first date, the anticipation is great, the first moment is nerve-wracking—and the first impression is critical, so prepare yourself for the big moment. You want the producer or editor to understand your story. Give the individual adequate time to review your material—then "smile and dial."

The first thing to consider is settling into a quiet, comfortable space. Background noises, music, or voices can be distracting to you as well as your phone contact. If you're going to spend a few hours at this, try a headset instead of a regular phone—it's easier to use.

Be organized, have your pitch letter and background data close at hand to refer to if you need it. Work from your media list and set up priorities. If this is your first time making follow-up calls, perhaps you want to start with a small paper or station because it will be less intimidating. Then go on by rank—either by size of audience or by deadline.

Do a practice run—use a friend or colleague as a role-player. Use a tape recorder and afterwards you can both critique the performance.

Did you sound:

♦ Nervous?

♦ Too pushy?

♦ Fake or rehearsed?

♦ Too loud?

♦ Too fast?

♦ Long and drawn out, never getting to the point?

♦ Unfocused?

♦ Enthusiastic and persuasive?

♦ As if you were listening as well as speaking?

♦ Friendly and easy to work with?

♦ Confident and concise?

Finally, prepare yourself by knowing exactly who you are talking to, the individual's job title and what that means. The person on the other end of the line should feel as if you have taken the time to understand their role first and you want them to understand your story.

What to say

Follow these six easy steps to secure the outcome you're looking for:

Step 1. Always identify yourself. Ask for someone specific.

Example dialogue: "Hi. This is John Smith calling from The Children's Rehabilitation Center. Would you put me through to Anita Bradford, the producer of the morning talk show?"

Step 2. Make sure it's a good time to talk.

Example dialogue: "Is now a good time to talk about the story idea I mailed to you?"

If it's not a good time, find out when is a good time. Ask for permission to call her back at a specific time and date.

Step 3. State clearly, concisely, and confidently why you are calling.

Example dialogue: "I'm calling to see if you would consider doing a story on the mathematical genius at The Children's Rehabilitation Center. The media kit I sent is a white pocket folder with a black-and-white photo of David on the front. Did you receive it?"

If your contact didn't receive your media kit, ask if you can explain more about the story. You want to make sure it makes sense to send the information. If it doesn't, you don't want to waste each other's time. If the contact wants the press kit, send it overnight or by messenger to communicate your urgency and conviction for the story.

Step 4. Offer suggestions, answer questions, and follow up.

Example dialogue: "I thought you might consider David for your 'Extraordinary Ordinaries' segment you do every Thursday morning. What do you think?"

Step 5: Diffuse objections by highlighting specifics.

If your contact says, "Thanks, but we did something similar to that two months ago. It might be too soon," try this:

"I saw that segment two months ago, which gave me the idea for this story. What makes this story different is he has a disability. Would that be of interest to your audience?" or "I admit I didn't see that segment two months ago. However, what makes this story unique is that David has a disability. Would that be of interest to your audience?"

If your contact says, "We do so many things like this. I don't see how yours is different," try this:

"David has a disability. He's also only 5 years old. He's solved a mathematical equation in less than a day that took the University of

Pennsylvania's top math students an entire semester to dissect. I have Penn students you can talk to about their experience with this little boy. He has courage and charm to go along with his special talent. Would that help to make the story different?"

If they say, "I'm not sure we have time to cover this. You're located all the way out by the airport," try this:

"If it's more convenient, David would be happy to come to the studio along with two Penn students. In addition, David will be receiving an award at the Hilton Hotel on Thursday, January 19 at 6 p.m. The Hilton is across the street from your studio. Perhaps you could get some footage there. "

Step 6: Ask about the next steps and confirm.

Example dialogue: "Where do we go from here, Ms. Bradford? Do you mind if I read this back to you so I know I have it correct? I will meet your reporters at the Hilton on Thursday, January 19 at 6 p.m. I'll have a table for them to hear David's speech. At 6:45, David and the reporters will have a private interview. I'll have two Penn students available for comment if necessary. Your reporters are welcome to stay for the reception, which starts at 7:30 p.m. I'll type this up and fax it to you if you don't mind. Looking forward to working with you and thanks."

It's your job to find out the needs of your contact (listen), match your story to these needs (know your source), alleviate fears (be prepared), and confirm the story (put closure to ensure commitment).

What if?

I get voice mail.

Leave a complete message specifying who you are, why you are calling, and when you will call back.

I've called five times and have gotten no response.

Keep trying. If your story is good, you'll get through. Don't assume they're avoiding your call—assume they are just very busy.

The editor/producer is rude.

Don't take it personally. Be friendly and sympathetic—they may be understaffed and overworked. Offer to call back.

They say that they didn't get my material (even if you're pretty sure it got through).

Perhaps it's been misplaced. They get a lot of mail. Tell them a little about your story, offer to send a new kit, and ask when you can call back.

They go off on a tangent.

Try, diplomatically, to get them back to your story by mentioning a specific aspect.

They ask about a topic outside of my expertise.

Don't try to be an expert where you are not—instead, offer a resource or referral.

They ask you to change the time of an event so that they can cover it.

Be flexible if you can—a short delay in exchange for a commitment may be fair.

Etiquette for pitching a story

♦ The media won't call you—calling them is part of the dance.

♦ Always ask if your contact is busy—be sensitive to the demands of the job.

♦ The media know you're calling to pitch an idea. Don't be bashful, apologetic, or overly chatty—get to the point.

♦ Never demand that a story runs—ask your contact to "consider" your story and use your charm and persuasion.

♦ Don't offer an exclusive and then run to book another station, as well.

♦ If one editor says no, don't pitch someone else in the same organization.

♦ Don't be coy and don't play games. If you have not sent a release and a deadline is approaching, admit your error.

♦ Pitch one story at a time.

Sometimes you succeed; sometimes you fail

If you've done your job well, and if your story is a good fit with the media source you've contacted, you'll most likely get a placement. Congratulations! Now, do your follow-up. Confirm the details in writing and send out any requested follow-up information right away. They may want an electronic media kit. Begin preparing your spokesperson (likely yourself) and everyone else who will be involved in the coverage.

What do you do if you strike out? Don't take it personally. If your story is good, the rejection is probably more about schedules and resources than you. And don't show your dissatisfaction. It won't change the fact that the story isn't going to run and you may damage a connection that could be valuable to you later on.

Be friendly and always say thank you for the consideration. Perhaps you can get some tips for your next story submission. Stay positive and know that there will be other opportunities in the future.

Chapter 9

Dress your elephant for the big show

Preparing for Your Interview

The first media call is always a thrill—it's a reporter, writer, or producer on the line wanting to talk about your favorite topic—*you*. The initial contact is usually to schedule the real moment—the interview. You've prepared your campaign and it's been a success. Now, get ready to become a media darling.

Each media format requires a slightly different emphasis but they do have similarities that you should keep in mind. The goal of all media is to entertain and educate as wide an audience as possible. They look for facts and accuracy and want you to be honest with them. The interview should be viewed as an extended conversation and your goal is to be perceived as credible, open, and friendly.

Print is for the eye and for keeps, it has details and texture. Radio is for the imagination—your audience will pick up on your attitude and fill in the blanks for themselves. Television is visual, so *how* you say something is as important as *what* you say. The Internet has the potential to combine everything—the visual, the audio, and, in some cases, it includes a level of interaction with the viewer as well.

Preparing for print

For all interviews, regardless of the medium, you need to take time to organize your thoughts and decide what points you want to get across. For radio and TV, you may be asked to come to a studio, so you will have some time to prepare. For print, this isn't a necessity and you may get a call from a reporter wanting to ask you a few questions at that moment. For beginners, unless you're very comfortable about an off-the-cuff interview, it is probably best to turn down the request and ask to set an appointment for a call-back or, better yet, an in-person conversation. Even if you have experience under your belt, you may choose to delay to have a chance to gather your thoughts and focus on the points you want to make.

If you can arrange to meet the reporter in person, try to make it at your office. Evan Pattak, former editor of *Executive Report Magazine* and a public relations consultant, suggests, "It's always useful if a writer sees you on your own turf." Who you are will be enhanced by the personal things on your desk or on your walls.

But make sure you can meet the reporter one-on-one. According to Pattak, "Other people can be a distraction," and in the end they will lessen your impact. Avoid interviews at restaurants—there's too much competition for the reporter's attention.

Create two or three talking points that highlight your story, and keep them inconspicuously on note cards so you can remind yourself of the focus. Role-play ahead of time so that working these into the conversation becomes natural.

Some reporters will ask to tape an interview. You may also want to bring a recorder of your own to assure you're properly quoted or even to learn how to improve your style.

Don't ask the reporter if you can approve the story before it runs; you know you won't get to and you will start off the interview by appearing suspicious. The best you can do is to offer your help in verifying any facts or details at any point. However, you should be sure to ask *when* the story will run and request copies.

Preparing for a radio interview

A radio interview can be done live or on tape; from your home or office, in the studio at a local station, or hundreds of miles away. No matter how or where, you *must*, in the words of Frank Gottlieb, a 20-year radio veteran and news director for the all-news KQV Radio in Pittsburgh, "know the station's format and focus before you begin."

Will you have five minutes during morning drive-time? Is the show taped in advance? The best way to find out about the format—if you didn't already learn this before you contacted the source—is to simply ask your contact at the radio station. Or if the placement was made through a publicist, they will be able to tell you.

The remote interview

You may be interviewed from your home or office on a remote call—you're hooked in via your phone line just as you would be if you were to call in to a talk show. The good news is that you will be in your own environment where you may feel more comfortable. The bad news is that when you can't see your questioner, it's harder to know when it's your cue to begin talking and you may run on a bit until the interviewer is forced to break in.

Take care to prepare a quiet place and be conscious of any background noise such as dogs, babies, music, and even traffic. Close the windows. Shut down your fax machine—the beeping is annoying. If you have call-waiting, disable it. Keep your notes where you can refer to them, and have a glass of water nearby in case you need it.

The station may arrange to call you a few minutes before the interview—or they may arrange to have you call them. Don't be surprised if you are asked to make the long-distance call—this is a common practice. If this is the case, be sure you confirm ahead of time any time differences. You will talk briefly to a producer and that is the time to ask for permission to mention a phone number or address and ask for a tape to be sent to you. Don't be alarmed or hurt if, after your interview, no one comes on to say thank you or good-bye. The fact that they are on the air demands that they move on to the next quest.

In the studio

Arrive on time for any interview—a little bit early will allow you a chance to get familiar with your surroundings. Don't be surprised that the radio studio is much smaller and less elegant than you may have expected. You will normally ask for the producer and he or she will come out to greet you and take you back to the studio to get you set up. Ask about the "cough button" in case you have to clear your throat (covering the mike with your hand won't do it). Don't touch any of the other equipment. Ask if you can have a glass of water in the studio in case your throat suddenly goes dry.

When you're on the air

Your personality will be transmitted by your voice—be upbeat and enthusiastic. Your passion and conviction will communicate over the airways. Some tips for success:

◆ Take your cue from your host or interviewer—pay close attention.

◆ Never interrupt when someone else is talking—it is annoying when no one can be heard.

◆ Don't be surprised by the introduction of controversy. Radio is a great format for diversity of opinions.

◆ If you're feeling attacked, take a deep breath and firmly change the subject.

- If you're part of a panel, give time to your fellow members and be assertive about getting your own equal share of the time.

- Don't try to cover up any lack of information, it will come through loud and clear. Be honest, say, "That's a good question, I'll have to look into that issue."

- If you're on a call-in show, don't worry about any obscene calls. Stations are on a seven- to 10-second delay and the engineer has experience in dealing with such calls. Chances are, they will never be heard by the audience.

How to prepare for a TV interview

A television interview, whether live or on tape, is a truly exciting event. It would be more unusual for you *not* to be a bit nervous. Remember, the more experience you get, the easier it will be.

Consider the fact that you are on a *visual* medium and pay attention to how you appear. This includes your attitude and energy level, as well as your physical image. Even if you feel stress, try to get a good sleep the night before. You'll appear more upbeat and you won't have bags under your eyes. Wear solid, bold colors and avoid small or busy prints. Men should button their jackets and sit on their coattails so their suit doesn't bunch up. Women should avoid revealing clothing and distracting jewelry—leave the big, flashy earrings at home.

Eat lightly before your interview—but do eat. A growling stomach can distract you and those around you. If you have anything to display, practice beforehand in front of a mirror or others. Make sure you know how to handle your material so your audience sees it at its best advantage and you don't look uncomfortable.

You may be doing your interview at the studio or on location. Regardless of the venue, you must prepare yourself for the questions to be asked and the information you wish to give. Settle on one theme and plan to keep your comments on point. If you start to wander, your audience will drift away, as well.

Try to meet the reporter in advance, even if it's just for a few minutes. If you have the time, ask any questions you might have about camera lights or commercial breaks. In some cases, you may get this information from the producer instead. Try to increase your own comfort level so that when the cameras start to roll, you'll look at ease.

An in-studio interview is a very structured environment. There will be a formal set and you will be told exactly where to stand or sit. They will also help you attach a microphone to your collar. On location, the surroundings are substantially looser. The crew is mobile (as few as one camera and a sound technician or as many as three or four people including a producer) and they won't decide where they are going to shoot until they get to the site. Even if it's your office, you probably won't know where you'll be sitting or standing until the on-site person decides. The good news in all of this is that you will likely have extra time with the reporter as the camera is being set up, so you can chat and get comfortable.

The toughest TV interview is the off-location remote—just you and a camera with a reporter only present via an audio feed in your earpiece. You must concentrate, anticipate the end of each question, and try to look comfortable in front of the camera. The best advice here is to treat the lens in front of your face as if it were another face—talk *with* it not *to* it. If you can see a camera person, perhaps you might talk to him or her.

Tips for when the cameras start rolling

♦ Sit or stand straight—keep your hands folded or at your side, not gesturing wildly.

♦ Don't fidget, don't itch, don't be frozen—try to relax.

♦ Never interrupt.

♦ Don't look at the camera. Talk to your questioner—make it look like conversation.

♦ Speak slowly and confidently.

♦ Nod only if you agree.

♦ The average report is no more than a minute or two. Make every second count.

♦ Don't hold papers—you'll rattle them and distract the audience.

More do's and don'ts on all media interviews

♦ Go with the flow, anything can happen.

♦ Always be *on*—off-the-cuff comments may be picked up and used.

♦ Don't drink alcohol before an interview. It won't calm you down and it may cause you to sweat or, worse yet, slur your words.

♦ Emphasize the positive—show your audience you believe in yourself and your business.

♦ Speak naturally.

♦ Relate to your audience in human terms.

♦ Enjoy yourself!

Internet interviews

There are basically two types of Internet interviews. One is the prepared question-and-answer session included on a Web site and the other is the interactive "guest chat," available on some sites.

The prepared interview may be very easy to do because questions will be submitted to you in advance and you will have sufficient time to compose your answers. Make sure your answers are short, to the point, and very clear. You will have a limited amount of space to make your points.

The "chat" interview is more difficult: It is done "live" with questions coming from all sorts of people who have logged on to the Web site. You may be surprised by some of them.

You can prepare yourself in two ways: First by doing all of your homework and having all the material you will need close by during the "chat." Before your interview, log on to as many of these sessions as you have time for so you can pick up on the rhythm and the most effective response format.

Finally, if you aren't a good typist, hire one to record your answers. No one will know and your typos won't be broadcast all over.

After the interview—show your appreciation

The end of the interview is not the end of the story for you. The members of the media that you meet along the way will play a role in your ongoing public relations success. Acknowledge your understanding of this by following up after you've been given the chance to tell your story. Say thank you!

Thank the people you worked with directly. Do it as soon as the story is out so they will be more likely to recognize your name. Most members of the media spend day-after-day meeting new people and weeks after a story has run, your name may have become a blur.

The best way to thank someone is in writing—a brief handwritten note is good. Also, a short note typed on your letterhead is appropriate. If you've had a particularly good experience and personally know someone in management, you could copy it to that person. Remember, the media outlet is a part of the business community, as well, and they like good public relations as much as you do.

If there was something special that you particularly liked about a print article, cut it out, copy it and highlight the section with a well-composed comment in the margin.

Don't go overboard with your compliments. Don't offer to take them to lunch unless you have developed a genuine rapport. Sending gifts is taboo, as well. Members of the media are conscious of their objectivity and don't want any hint of favoritism. Finally, do not drop by the station again just to say thanks. You've seen how hectic it can become and you should show that you respect this reality.

Taking the time and making the effort to send your thanks will cast you as a true professional and a pleasure to work with—that's an image that will pay off later.

Chapter 10

Tearing your tutu at the last minute

When Things Go Wrong During the Interview

Not all interviews go smoothly, not all programs go as planned, and some don't come off at all. The best-laid plans can go off course at the last minute. Whenever you go into the arena of the media, expect the unexpected and be prepared to handle any surprises like a pro. You will be noticed for your grace and good humor in these instances, and your professional behavior will put you in a good light for the future.

There are an infinite number of things that can go wrong, but some situations tend to be more common than others, and foreseeing such circumstances and preparing for appropriate response is a wise course of action. What follows are some of the more frequent circumstances you might face, with suggestions for dealing with them. A short, real-life "Lessons learned" scenario is included for further illustration of the principles offered.

What if...

Your name or other key information is mispronounced or just plain wrong?

You can...

Try to prevent this before it happens. If you have a difficult name to pronounce, include a pronunciation guide in your press release and all print materials. Just prior to the interview, say it clearly to the interviewer and perhaps joke about how it's often botched up.

If your interviewer makes a mistake, be polite but correct it as soon as you can. If you wait until the misinformation is repeated several times, you'll both look foolish.

If you are close to a commercial break, wait and point out the correction off the air.

Lesson learned

Carole Barnes is an aggressive, young Midwestern marketing consultant, offering advice to nonprofit agencies on positioning themselves for the future. While serving on a radio panel, the host referred to her as Carla Burns, who was actually the executive director at one of the city's large agencies. In response, Carole corrected her interviewer good-naturedly by saying, "It's flattering to be confused with Carla, she's one of my heroes. Her agency long ago learned how to change to respond to the needs of the community and that's what I'm trying to teach my clients in the seminar we're conducting this weekend." It was seamless.

What if...

You're asked a personal question that makes you uncomfortable?

You can...

Brush it off gently and revert back to your topic. For example, "I haven't given a lot of thought to that, but one of the issues that does concern me is..."

Even if you are offended by the question, don't get defensive. A response such as, "That's none of your business," although perhaps legitimate, will result in your looking as if you have something to hide, even if you don't.

Lesson learned

Pennsylvania State Senator Melissa Hart was a guest on a live radio call-in show about the financing of a new stadium in Pittsburgh. Hart, who supported a lottery-financed strategy, was fielding tough questions from interested callers. Out of the blue, the host asked, "Is it true you're dating Kevin McClatchey?" (McClatchey is the owner of the Pittsburgh Pirates). Although this had been rumored, it was clear by her pause that she wasn't expecting the question. With the finesse of a politician, she deflected the question saying, "Sounds like our listeners would rather hear about saving money than my love life and there are two more tax-saving points I'd like to make before my time is up."

What if...

There is a compelling reason why you can't show for your interview?

You can...

Call as soon as you know you can't make the interview. Be sure to offer an alternative spokesperson, if you have one available. And be available to reschedule at the interviewer's convenience.

Sometimes we can't control events that render us incapable of meeting our obligations: illnesses that leave us hoarse and sneezing; a delayed flight or missed connection; a car that breaks down or traffic congestion. The first course of action is to do everything you can to *prevent* such occurrences. Schedule plenty of extra time, for example, to get to the interview in case there are airport or traffic delays. Have a back-up babysitter in case your childcare arrangements go awry.

But when you've lost the battle against the flu, or some other force is keeping you from meeting the interview time, then you owe it to the interviewer to communicate this as soon as possible, so that contingency plans can be made.

Lesson learned

A new young writer, on his first book tour, found himself in city number-three with a terrible cold and growing fatigue. He had several radio shows to do to promote a lecture and bookstore appearance. Calls to the producer changed his in-studio shots to remotes from his hotel room—his bed to be exact. He saved his energy and the producers filled their air time.

What if...

You spill food on your neatly starched white shirt a few minutes before going on live TV?

You can...

Change into your backup shirt that you wisely brought with you.

Again, plan in advance for such situations. First, don't eat spaghetti or any other messy foods just before your interview. Or wear a bib if you insist on doing so. Yet if the inevitable happens, a backup ensemble will come in handy. A final possibility? You might ask if you can borrow a jacket or shirt—those in front of the camera often have changes of clothing for themselves on hand. Although, asking the news anchor if you can wear his clothing may prove more embarrassing than appearing on TV with a stain on your shirt.

Lesson learned

During the Children's Miracle Network Telethon, a local celebrity radio announcer was waiting to go on television, a different medium for him, when he inadvertently spilled a full cup of coffee on his shirt and he wasn't wearing a jacket. With seconds to spare, the son of another guest who was waiting in the green room, stripped off his shirt and gave it to the celebrity who in turn handed him his wet, coffee-soaked garment. The celebrity went on and actually used the incident to poke fun at himself and make the guest's son out to be a hero.

What if...

Time is running out and you haven't said near enough about your main topic?

You can...

Prepare a one- or two-line teaser in advance to use in just such a situation. Leave your interviewer and your audience wanting more. Rehearse a great closing that covers what you consider your most important points (this may include a toll-free phone number or other information that allows the audience to get in touch with you) and, when you sense that time is almost up, you can be prepared to slip this statement in.

Lesson learned

While promoting Valentine's Day gift ideas, the owner of a lingerie shop felt that the show host had carefully kept the program from turning into a free commercial. Understanding that, she still wanted the opportunity to attract customers to *her* store. Her last point was presented this way: "You know, some men still are embarrassed by buying ladies' lingerie. That's why we have a 'men only' night on February 11th complete with models and wine and cheese. We want your man to shop in comfort." Enough said!

What if...

You are asked a question outside of your area of expertise and knowledge?

You can...

Be honest and admit you don't know. Never let this sort of admission dangle. Admit you don't know the answer but veer into an area that you are strong in. For example, if you've written a city guidebook and the interviewer asks how many Italian restaurants there are, you might say, "I can't tell you that, but I do know that no matter what part of town you live in, you're surrounded by a selection of excellent Italian restaurants that offer a range of prices and menus."

Lesson learned

In the midst of the heightened public interest in health care reform, many hospital groups sent spokespeople to represent them on radio and TV panels. One hospital administrator took a call from an anxious listener wanting to know how this health care provider would handle upcoming surgery at the administrator's facility. Not knowing the exact answer, an offer was made to the caller to find out the specifics and get back to him. The sincere tone of the administrator's offer diffused an emotionally charged area of discussion.

What if...

The entire topic of the show is altered at the last minute?

You can...

If you are part of a panel and the focus has changed to meet breaking news, you may suggest that you are not an appropriate guest and offer to reschedule.

If you are already into an interview and the topic gets way off track, do your best to redirect it. Make a brief comment about the "new" topic, and then move on to an intriguing statement within your area of expertise.

Lesson learned

A psychologist offering a program on career planning was scheduled on a radio show the morning after a tragic incident of workplace violence. The show host opened the segment with an overview of the tragedy and proceeded to ask his guest how workers can spot the potential violence in their co-workers. While the guest had expertise on human behavior, this was totally outside of her area and she expressed sympathy to the victims of the violence and quickly directed the conversation back to career choices.

What if...

Your hot story is canceled from TV because of a major local or national event?

You can...

Acknowledge the proper sense of priorities and be ready to re-schedule. You might use this delay to reposition your story for an even bigger launch. Try to set a new date on the spot. If you can't, then be sure to call back or write a note to the producer as soon as possible, in order to reschedule your interview.

Lesson Learned

Bumping a public relations story for a major event of public interest is standard procedure and sometimes, the circumstances can be quite ironic. USAir was staging a media conference to announce a new product called "Business Select," aimed at attracting more frequent flyers. Executives were in town and the press had been alerted. On that same day, the news was preempted by the tragic crash of USAir Flight 427 into a hill outside of Pittsburgh, killing all on board. Some things are really more important.

Chapter 11

Turn it around when your tutu is down

Getting Media Attention for the *Wrong* Reasons

As exciting as it is to hear from the media in response to a press release, there may be a time when the last thing in the world you want is to hear from a reporter. For whatever reason—perhaps because of a customer complaint, dishonest practices of a competitor or related business, or negative press on your industry as a whole—their are times when bad press seems to follow you.

You've seen it happen to large companies—the disaster of a crash, financial meltdown ending in bankruptcy, medical emergencies caused by tainted products, or a myriad of unplanned events that create a feeding frenzy among the media. And you've seen how these "situations" have been handled: the ones that have grown into a public relations nightmare as well as the companies that have turned a negative into a positive.

The case most often used as an example of the right thing to do when caught in the middle of public relations crisis? The Tylenol incident. The episode began when it was discovered that some Tylenol tablets had been laced with cyanide, which caused several deaths. The manufacturer had nothing at all to do with this tragedy and it was clear early in the case that it was the singular act of an outside individual. Regardless, the company acted quickly and brilliantly.

Before the day had come to an end, the CEO had called a press conference and made a public announcement that all product would be taken off the shelves while an investigation was conducted. Further, he said that no new product would be sold until a higher level of protection was created. For many weeks, no Tylenol was available to the public, a move that was risky given that customers could make other pain relief choices during that time. Many wondered whether Tylenol would ever recapture their share of the market again.

When the launch of the redesigned tamper-proof packaging was announced, not only did it set new standards for an entire industry, it set the stage for one of the most impressive product come-backs of all time. The public level of trust in Tylenol and its manufacturer actually went up as a result of this crisis.

Your company isn't very likely to experience a challenge of this magnitude, but for many small businesses, the after-effect of any negative publicity can be disastrous. Tylenol's manufacturer was so successful with their public relations effort because it had plan in *advance* to respond to any emergency. You need not create a full scale plan, such as the one in place by Tylenol's manufacturer, but you should give some consideration about how you would handle yourself in a crisis.

What would you do if you operated a catering business and there was an outbreak of food poisoning? Or a bridal shop that had a burst frozen pipe destroying the gowns for a wedding less than a week away? Or a foreign car auto repair having four classic cars destroyed by fire? No business owner expects disaster, but keeping the public informed and maintaining confidence may be the determining factor in the future of the company.

Take action when faced with bad press

When you suddenly find yourself in the midst of bad publicity, you may fear that your business is coming to a grinding halt. You may begin to wonder if the whole world is out to get you and be overwhelmed and overextended by the situation. You will probably wish that the problem and everyone associated with it would just go away.

These reactions are natural. But to ignore the situation and wait for it to "go away" is almost always the wrong thing to do. The following are steps to take when confronted by a crisis.

1. Enlist a group of friendlies. Now more than ever, you need a support team. If your company has good ongoing relationships with a group of professionals—an attorney, accountant, marketing or public relations consultant (now is when you may wish you had a tutu expert), and a financial advisor—now is the time to call them together. If there are key inside people who would make good team members, bring them along, as well. Perhaps a few trusted business associates can be included to add objective outside opinions.

2. Tell your employees everything that you intend to make public. Help them understand what has happened from your perspective so that if asked, they won't undermine the company position. All employees need to be informed of what to say and what not to say, or how to direct inquiries. It's best to direct employees *not* to answer any media questions, but to have them referred to the appropriate spokesperson.

3. Make sure you have all of the facts and the supporting documentation, as well. Double-check for accuracy and keep it all in one place so you can access any document easily. If there are charges or lawsuits that are public record, the last thing you want to do is give inaccurate information that can be checked.

4. Focus on the crisis, but don't let other business go. Delegate as much of your work and projects as possible to others that you trust. Crisis management is a full-time challenge. If there is any way you can put your full-time attention to it, by all means do so.

5. Communicate with your customers as soon as possible. Describe the problem as fully as you can, whether it's a product failure, a financial failure, a pending investigation, or any controversial situation that has already or may soon become public knowledge. Your words will serve to minimize the impact and show that you are in control and likely to overcome the problem. Be positive about the plans you are making or steps you are taking to correct the situation. For any long-term situation, send out progress bulletins along the way. It is critical to maintain your customer base. Misinformation may undermine confidence.

6. Don't forget about your family. They are probably worried and want to be supportive of you. Even if you're up to your ears in alligators, you need them and they you. Don't lose your humanity in the midst of a crisis. Keep your family as informed as you keep staff and customers informed. They're your PR to the neighborhood, community, and schools. Set aside time for them, whether a weekend family event, or a quiet dinner. A publicity crisis can sometimes steal all your personal time.

7. Be accessible. Keep a pager or cell phone with you. Give all pertinent individuals your number and be as accessible as possible. If you are the only spokesperson for the company and you aren't available, information gaps will develop. Nature abhors a vacuum, so silence will be filled by misinformation. Don't let this happen.

8. Be prepared for the media. Try to anticipate their questions and prepare yourself with all the information you can get.

What to do when the media arrives

If the crisis is big enough, interesting enough, or if an individual decides to blow the whistle, you may find yourself face-to-face with a reporter—or a whole pack of them. With proper anticipation, you should be as well-prepared for them as possible.

Here are some tips to win the day.

- ◆ Center yourself and remain calm.

- ◆ When the call comes in, respond immediately. This is one reason you are wearing a beeper. If you delay, the impression will be that you are being secretive and stonewalling for enough time to cover up.

- ◆ Play out the worst-case scenarios in your head and anticipate the tough questions and your responses as well. Determine all the positives and make sure you include them in your answers.

- ◆ Offer all of the facts you can and emphasize those that tend to shine the most positive light on your current situation as well as your overall business.

- ◆ Answer what has been asked as completely as you can. Don't go off on a tangent and give too much information. Remember, it will be distilled for the public consumption and you want to be sure that they hear the important information.

- ◆ Don't hide—meet the challenge head on.

♦ Avoid saying "no comment" unless your lawyer demands that you do. It has a nasty ring to it. As a last resort, say, "We're still gathering all the facts and will have a statement as soon as we're done. We appreciate your patience."

♦ Don't appear to be indignant at even the most inappropriate question. Change the subject or, if you have the skill, turn it around with humor. Any show of negative emotion can be turned against you.

♦ Don't be afraid. Don't give your power to the media—if you believe you have what it takes to turn this crisis around, you will.

♦ Don't overdramatize or overhype. Be concise and stick with the facts.

♦ Don't pass the ball to someone else. If it's your problem, show the courage to accept the responsibility.

♦ Stand tall even when you feel weak. Show courage and leadership. Act if you have to—you'll have time to let down with friends and family. The storm will pass and you will earn respect with your ability to weather it.

♦ When it's over, let it go.

You can emerge as a hero

When a Massachusetts textile company went up in flames in early winter of 1996, totally destroying the plant and creating major unemployment, the news coverage was initially of a community tragedy. But then the owner came forward to say that he would re-build the plant as quickly as possible in the same town, thereby saving an important source of jobs. He also committed to paying wages to employees out of his own pocket for 30 days as a sign of his appreciation of the past effort and loyalty of his workforce. The 30 days stretched into several months but the rebuilding went smoothly and limited production resumed sooner than expected. The national press picked up this story and both the owner and the workers were featured on the evening news, news magazines, and national publications as American heroes. The genuine affection and respect between owner and workers was a business triumph that emerged from a tragedy.

If you show courage, leadership, and some measure of grace under pressure, perhaps you, too, can emerge as a hero.

Use a crisis to show your commitment to quality and service

The Tylenol tragedy became a positive for the company because the public perceived how much the product's manufacturer really cared about the safety of its customers. By withdrawing all of the product from all shelves when the incident was limited to one state, the message that quality was more important than profits was sent all over the country. It is the kind of positive image any company would love to have.

If your crisis is over the quality of your product, take all the extra steps you can to rectify the situation and try to assure everyone in every way that your commitment is to be ahead of the curve in exceptional quality and service.

Let your personality win the day

If you have a natural ability to charm, entertain, or amuse, don't be afraid to poke fun at yourself (if the problem you are dealing with hasn't caused injury or other harm to others). Laughing at yourself can be the most effective way of humanizing your company and winning greater fans and new customers. Looking around at his waterlogged, mud-soaked restaurant recently flooded by an over-flowing river, the owner quipped, "Until now, I didn't know we had a seaside view."

When all else fails...chalk it up to experience

Sometimes a crisis comes on so swiftly and intensely that even a trained professional may not have known how to diffuse it. You do what you can do. Don't regret your efforts even if they haven't been totally successful. Don't hold grudges. Learn from it, forget it and move on.

When it's over

Now is the time to enhance what you've done right and learn from everything that has happened. If you have received positive coverage, by all means circulate it as widely as possible. Send copies to employees and customers with a personal note of thanks for their patience, their efforts, and their support. Once again, reiterate your personal commitment to go forward.

Evaluate your crisis communication plan and make any changes you feel are needed. If you had to call in the services of a profes-sional (an attorney or public relations consultant, for example), make sure you maintain your relationship, should these services be needed again. Ask for and accept feedback from those who have been in-volved, particularly employees and customers. Be open to sugges-tions and learn from your own mistakes.

If any member of the media was particularly helpful and even-handed in their reporting, take the time to send a note. They will ap-preciate the fact that you understand.

Chapter 12

One-size-fits-all tutus

Great Ideas for Any Business

Good public relations means more to the success of your company than pitching stories to the media for an occasional article or appearance. Raising public awareness about you, your company, and your product or service is one key element in a successful marketing strategy. What you want to do on a consistent basis is circulate the name, product, or image of your business in a way that best brings positive awareness. There are many good ideas—here are some that have worked for others and may work for you.

1. Create a tip sheet or booklet with valuable advice that you offer free to customers, readers, and listeners.

- Mention this free information in every interview. If it's free, many media outlets will give out the details of how to contact you.

- It allows you to hear from people who can be potential prospects for your business.

- It helps you build a mailing list for future marketing.

- You can put it on your Web site as another means of collecting prospect information.

2. Mount and frame your articles for your office.

♦ It creates an instant image of credibility.

♦ It allows people to get to know you better.

♦ Have copies available on a coffee table for the taking—include your contact information.

♦ If you see a colleague or client in the media, get the story mounted for them, too. It makes a memorable and inexpensive gift.

3. Turn your seminars into topics for a radio call-in show.

♦ List the most frequently asked questions from your seminar and use them as your format for the show.

♦ Be able to provide guests who have attended your seminar as part of a panel.

♦ It helps to promote future seminars and positions you as an expert in your field.

♦ You can use the format as the outline to create audio tapes for sale.

4. Use *Chase's Calendar of Events* (found in any library) to create your own public relations event. It contains thousands of special days, weeks, months, and anniversaries (some wacky, some profound), and trivia to tie in to your publicity efforts. The book is indexed by title and key words. Makes a great desk reference for the publicity hound.

♦ For example, "Be Good to Yourself Week" starts January 18—perfect for beauty salons and spas to use as a promotional event.

♦ "Be Late for Something Day" is September 5—time management seminar leaders could use this as a hook.

♦ The Beatle's last album was released on September 26— record stores can tie this in to sales promotions.

♦ The All-American Pet Photo Day is July 11— veterinarians could hire a photographer and take photos of pets and their owners; photographers could use it as a hook to bring families and pets in.

5. Write op-ed pieces for publications in your field or industry.

♦ It could be a first-person viewpoint of "a day in the life," sharing the challenges you've faced and the solutions to overcome them.

♦ Peers in your area can learn from your experiences. Doesn't matter if you're a CPA, an attorney, or a physician. All fields have industry periodicals appropriate for this type of message.

6. Become actively involved in a cause, charity, or nonprofit organization.

♦ Donate your product or service to an event such as a charity auction or door-prize giveaway.

♦ Buy uniforms for a youth sports team. (Your logo or name typically appears on the shirt.)

♦ Volunteer to be on the board of a nonprofit organization. (It's a great way to meet other business leaders and perhaps even make media contacts.)

♦ Sponsor a fund-raising event. (This means that your company name may appear on all promotional materials and advertising for the event.)

7. Come up with an irresistible name for your business, product, seminars, or concept.

♦ The media loves a good name, they can play it up.

♦ It helps people to connect to and remember you.

8. Find ways to use a client or a customer in your public relations pitches. (Word-of-mouth referrals are some of the best marketing vehicles available.)

♦ When you're putting together your next pitch, think of ways to include people related to your business. It promotes goodwill, and the people you use will sing your praises.

♦ List some great testimonials on your promotional brochure.

♦ Build a "referral" list of clients willing to share their positive experiences with others.

9. Send a letter on your letterhead and a business card to key media contacts alerting them that you can serve as a resource at any time.

♦ Make sure you bullet-point your areas of expertise. They may keep your name on file and use you in a pinch.

♦ Include your home phone and/or beeper number to give the perception that you are available at any time, day or night.

♦ It's a subtle way to introduce yourself to the media. They may be inclined to remember your name when you send a press release in the future.

10. Host an outrageous free event.

♦ Do this only if it is appropriate for the image of your business.

♦ Howard Stern decided to run for mayor of New York, which gave him tremendous, albeit controversial, publicity.

♦ Jack Canfield and Mark Victor Hansen, authors of the "Chicken Soup" series, gave a copy of their book to everyone on a plane and hired a photographer to take a photo of everyone reading it. The caption said, "Look what everybody is reading" and was published in many major periodicals across the country.

♦ Hire a skywriter and create promotional interest for people to watch for "a secret message in the sky."

♦ Hold a Christmas sale in July and dress appropriately.

♦ Outrageous and fun themes help to fill space and air time and it gives you free mentions.

11. Broadcast, fax, or send an online newsletter with a tip of the week, month, or day.

♦ If the media is on your list, every once in a while they may use one of your tips if they are appropriate to their readers, listeners, and viewers.

♦ It's a way to constantly keep your name in front of people and it's giving them something of value.

♦ It's a sure-fire way to begin positioning yourself as an expert in a particular field.

12. Step back in time.

♦ Let the media and your customers know you're selling a product at 1940s pricing. Have someone there, a senior from the community, who can verify the price and talk about "the way it used to be." Decorate accordingly. Publish a history of your neighborhood or area. Find photos that show how it has changed over time.

♦ This tactic gets people thinking about their communities. The history of a community is of particular interest to the residents. It will help them to remember you as well.

13. Take advantage of "done deals."

♦ There are certain publications that will publish just about anything you send them. Take advantage of that. It could include your chamber of commerce newsletter, alumni newsletters and magazines from your college, high school, trade school. Send information to the newsletters of the organizations to which belong. Send a photo whenever you can.

14. Prepare and rehearse a strong 30-second soundbite about your business. This is your concise, one- to two-sentence description of who you are, what you do, and the benefit you provide to your clients/customers. It's how you want to become known and famous.

♦ In addition to putting it in every press release that goes out, put it on your stationery, fax sheets, fliers, brochures, video and audio tapes, advertisements, and as part of your trade show booth. Say it in all interviews. Display it on your counters or in the window of your store. Everywhere you can think of—be creative, be consistent, and don't be afraid to shout it from the mountaintops.

♦ People will begin to make the association with you and certain key words and will start to think of you first before the competition.

15. Get media calendars from key media sources and find a way to fit in. Every print media source should have a calendar of what they plan to do for the year. Simply call and they can send this information to you.

♦ For example, every year, your local business publication may do a health care supplement in May. If you run a group practice, or a billing company, plan to make a presence. Serve as a resource to the media for these special promotions. But don't overdo it.

16. Write a column/host a show.

♦ Especially for local newspapers, submit a proposal to write a column in your area of expertise, particularly if you see a gap in that area. An interior designer submitted a proposal to a local TV station and ended up with her own spot every Wednesday morning to give tips on home comfort and decorating. She's becoming famous in her own town, which is exactly what she wanted in the first place.

17. Sponsor an unusual contest or award.

♦ You may not have to go through the process of collecting a large number of entries. You can select and announce the recipient who was chosen by a panel if you wish to do so. Best and worst are entertaining as long as they're understood to be tongue-in-cheek. You don't want to ruin anyone's reputation.

18. Do some research and publish your own study.

♦ Have questionnaires at the counter of your store; ask people informally how they feel about timely issues. Send the results to the media.

19. Piggyback on current news. There are many ways to get free publicity based on the news of the day as long as you're offering information that is valuable to the recipient.

♦ For example, in the midst of a natural disaster, an insurance agent could publish the five things you must not overlook to make sure you're covered in a disaster.

♦ If unemployment rates are high or if an employer lays off hundreds of people, a career counselor can speak about the first thing you must do when you are laid off.

♦ Many grief therapists shared their viewpoint on how to cope with grief after the death of Princess Diana.

....

Chapter 13

Advice from the ringmaster

Frequently Asked Questions About PR

Throughout the previous chapters, we've developed a step-by-step plan that any business can follow to create and implement a public relations strategy. Once you've digested all of the material, you should be ready to go. If you still need to fill in some of the blanks, the following frequently asked questions and their answers are provided here as an easy reference tool and to emphasize key information.

Q: How do I develop story ideas to attract the media to my area of expertise?

A: Try putting a new spin on a current topic. For example, some public relations consultants tell their clients to keep two lists nearby. One is marked "Trends," and the other is marked "Client Questions." Keep track of important trends in your target industry on one, and make a list of all client questions on the other. After a week or so, categorize the results. This way, you'll know trends better than reporters, who may find your insights valuable.

Q: What's the difference between public relations and marketing?

A: Public relations is a marketing tool just like advertising, special events, and direct mail are marketing tools. A successful public relations campaign sets the stage for the balance of your marketing plan but it must not replace the rest of your efforts. Marketing is about creating awareness and opportunities. The more targeted components such as advertising and direct mail are equally important.

Q: What does the media look for in deciding on story ideas?

A: Basically, the news must have a unique slant to it. It must appeal to audience or readership of a particular media source. Aviva Radbord, public affairs director and weekend assignments editor for KDKA-TV2 in Pittsburgh, has been assigning and developing story ideas for more than 20 years. She says a good story "must appeal to people on an emotional level. The best stories affect thousands of people's lives; they're meaningful, and leave a lasting impression." Adds Dan Bates, editor of the *Small Business News* in Pittsburgh, "What attracts my attention is that it must be a compelling story that addresses a certain issue very specifically. The topic must meet the interests of our reader and the focus of our publication." In addition, "Exclusivity is a big part of it," says another newspaper editor. "That makes good news, particularly if we're promised we'll have it first."

Q: I published one article—now what?

A: Contribute to charity, donate merchandise, give a speech, open a new business, move a business location, take on a leadership position, announce an anniversary, host an unusual special event, offer free programs, take a stand on an issue, solve a crisis, add new staff, publish a book, reveal an unusual hobby, serve as a resource, win an award, publish research results, sponsor a team/tournament/float in a parade. The list is endless. Be creative and keep your antenna up for ongoing opportunities.

Q: Can you boil the public relations game down to five easy steps?

A: In short, here are five steps to free publicity:

1. Define who you are and what you do.
2. Create a picture of how you are different.
3. Create a story about you and put it in press release format.
4. Compile a targeted media list.
5. Release it to the media and follow up.

Q: How do I compile a media list?

A: For local media, you can contact your chamber of commerce. For regional, national, and international resources, there are many books available (listed in the resource section of this book). If you are online, there are a number of Internet sites to use as a resource.

Q: At what point do I need a professional?

A: Refer to Chapter 5 of this book for a complete discussion of this topic. However, in short, the three issues to consider are time, complexity, and expense of your publicity effort. If you don't have the time, are a stranger to the particular media market, and have the funds available, you have come to the point that a professional is a viable option.

Q: What are the major no-no's in developing a public relations campaign?

A: Never start without a written plan and goals. Never, ever misspell a media contact's name. Never pitch a story to a media source you don't know anything about. Never forget to explain the who, what, where, when, and why of your story for the media. Never call the media just before deadline or minutes before they're going live on the air.

Q: How do I evaluate whether my public relations campaign is a success?

A: Evaluating your public relations campaign is more than just a numbers game. There are many questions you need to answer in order to ensure the success of your public relations activities. You should have goals before you launch any effort:

1. How much media exposure did our campaign generate? This could be determined by totaling the number of articles published and the "reach" or readership of each.

2. Are we really reaching our target audience? An article published is great, but if no one in your target audience is reading it, is it really worth your effort?

3. Is our key message getting across? With proper planning and carefully constructed press releases and interviews, you should be able to get your message across masterfully.

4. Is the press responding favorably to our publicity? The headline says it all. A short glance through your clippings will tell you if the press has been negative or positive. Hopefully, for you, it's always positive.

Q: What should I keep in mind when I'm being interviewed by the press?

A: Evan Pattak, former editor of *Executive Report Magazine* and a widely respected veteran of public relations says, "Everybody has an agenda." You want to promote your business and the media wants to entertain and enlighten their readers. "It's important to establish up front some points of congruence," says Pattak. "Align your interests," he says. Then, everybody wins. From a broader perspective, most serious media people, veterans or not, understand the impact the media has on people's lives. Their mission is to get it right.

Q: Should I let a reporter tape-record the interview?

A: As a rule, most reporters do tape their interviews to make sure they quote you properly and to ensure accuracy in the content. Pattak has conducted thousands of interviews and says that in most cases, it may be awkward at first, as most people are not used to being taped. However, in a matter of minutes, if the reporter is good, both parties get so involved in the interview that the recorder is forgotten. It's important to agree up front that taping will take place.

Q: What are some of the pet peeves of the media?

A: Here's a sampling:

1. A guest is booked for a show and at the time of the taping, the individual shows up with another guest, and wants this person on the show, too. "We usually can't do it," says KDKA-TV's Aviva Radbord, and the guest leaves unhappy because of bad judgment or lack of knowledge of the process of television.

2. Someone does not work through the proper channels to try to get a guest on a show. In the words of another television producer, "There's some public relations people who will only talk to the host and not to the producer, even when the proper protocol is to work directly with the producer. That simply muddies the waters when it comes to scheduling. Something is going to get lost in the transition."

3. Individuals seeking publicity pester media representatives at home. Says Harvey Kart, editor of *Hospital News*, "People will look my name up in the phone book and call me at night when I'm having dinner with my family. There are a few privileged individuals who actually have my home phone number. Otherwise, if I don't give it out, I don't want the call."

4. Interviewees are often unprepared for their interview. A legal expert was invited to share her expertise about a high-profile case on a TV panel. She did little or no research on the trial being discussed, and prefaced all of her answers with, "I don't know much about the specifics of this case, but generally..." The rest of the panel was visibly annoyed.

5. Faxing unnecessary elements is another annoyance. Frank Gottlieb, news director for KQV radio and who has been in the business for 22 years, says they go through a roll of fax paper a day mostly because people send the "to and from" cover sheet on a separate page. "The best way to send a fax is to forget about the cover and put the "to and from" in the top right-hand corner of the page using a transmittal sticker. There's no need for a separate cover page." In addition, a pet peeve is faxing 10 pages or more. "Send it in the mail if it's that long. When faxes stack up, we might ignore a 10-page fax because it's too time-consuming to read. Plus it ties up our machines."

6. Callers often follow up a press release mailing, asking, "Did you get my press release?" Most media contacts are buried in stacks of paper and piles of press releases. Don't expect them to remember yours as if it were the only one. Start your call by telling them of the value of your story, then follow by telling them that you sent a press release. Your intro is likely to trigger their memory regarding the press release.

7. People ask to review an article before it goes to press or the tape before it goes on the air. There's a universally accepted principle that the media has the last word. They print or air what they determine should be printed or aired.

Q: Could you describe a day in the life of the media?

A: Every media outlet is different. Overall, it can be stressful because, in most cases, you can't anticipate breaking news and what it will take to report it accurately. For television, the day may be split up between assignment work, taping, and looking for good new story ideas. They may be responding to urgent information. For radio, a news director may start the day by catching up on what happened since leaving the previous day, particularly major stories. He or she may coordinate the operation of 15 or more staff to do stories for the day, sending someone to a scene of breaking news, or to do a story from a press release received. Phone calls are fielded. It never stops. Lunch is usually eaten at the desk. Before the day ends, the next day's schedule will be reviewed to see which news events are planned.

For print, "We are only as good as the information flow," says newspaper editor Dan Bates. "You have to be out there talking to sources. You have to be on lots of mailing lists. Information is who we are." Therefore, Bates spends a great deal of time sifting through information to uncover stories. He uses a system to save as much time as possible. "I'm inundated every day with information. If I have to read more than the headline and the first few sentences to understand what it's about, I usually don't read any further. I simply don't have the time." If he's not searching, he's writing, interviewing, editing other reporters' work, assigning stories for the week, or fielding phone calls.

Most media have less resources to work with. They require strict planning and quick turnaround time. They never know what news is going to break next. The more information you can provide them, the better. In addition, keep in mind that the media is always looking to do "the next story." It could be yours.

Q: How does the media feel about public relations consultants (tutu experts) pitching my story on my behalf?

A: For every media contact, you will get varying answers, depending on their experience with public relations consultants. Most have had good and bad experiences. "It depends on the client and who they decide to represent," says radio news director Frank Gottlieb. "Many times, public relations consultants allow the client to dictate what gets sent out. Many times it's not relevant, and it comes over the wire all the time. Apparently the client isn't being educated by their public relations consultant. Sometimes less is more. More can be annoying, particularly if it's simply to show that 'something' is being sent. You'll find diminishing returns after a while of sending nonusable information."

Q: What's the best way to send information to the media?

A: The best way to pitch a story is still by fax or mail. All media contacts have their preferences. For breaking news, faxing is probably the fastest way. "There's always someone walking past the fax machine," says one radio station manager. However, as technology takes a leap, our media may be accepting more and more information electronically.

Q: I've called the media several times to follow up on a press release and all I get is voice mail. Should I leave a message?

A: Most media contacts will have a pile of pink slips on their desk to return phone calls. If you've tried several times and can't get through, leave a message. However, says newspaper editor Dan Bates, "Leave a compelling reason for me to call you back." Persistence will pay off in the end.

....

Chapter 14

The elephant in the pink tutu...

Conclusion

You have chosen to read this book because you want a higher degree of public appreciation for your business and its products or services. You know that the media can do a lot for you—open doors, obtain new clients, impress strangers. But perhaps you still wonder if it can happen to you.

If you need any inspiration, look back at the stories of the management consultant who got media coverage for his free seminars, and Lucille Treganowan, owner of Transmissions by Lucille and the car clinic guru, in Chapter 3. You can learn from others in Chapter 10, like Carole Barnes who aced a radio interview or the retail store owner who took advantage of the media's ability to promote Valentine's Day sales.

The most memorable media stories will be those involving you. Go out there and create a memory! If you have success stories you would like to share, please write to:

Cronin Communications
709 Tally Drive
Pittsburgh, PA 15237
800-798-4702   (fax) 800-798-4703
E-mail: MMC@aol.com
Web site: http://www.cyberscoreinc.com/cronin

Appendix 1

Sample Publicity Plan

The following is an example of a Publicity Plan Format.

Innovative Financial Services

A. Goal: To conduct a publicity campaign from November 1997 to November 1998 to achieve greater public awareness for Innovative Financial Services.

Brief background: Client base for Innovative Financial Services consists of small business owners and small privately held companies, primarily in the Western Pennsylvania region.

B. Key Angle:

♦ Charitable Gift Funds—an alternative to achieving philanthropic goals.

C. & D. Media outlets and contact information databases:

Charitable Gift Funds—story (with photo of principle of company)

♦ Western Pennsylvania TV, radio, and print media—financial editors specifically.

♦ 300 databases and online services (including the Dow Jones News Retrieval).

♦ The Investor's Resource Wire.

♦ Trade publications (list specifically).

♦ Disclosure media (*The Wall Street Journal, The New York Times*).

♦ 2,500 business and financial editors of print, radio, TV across the country (list specifically in database).

♦ 100,000 terminals of investors and analysts.

- ♦ Releases posted on our own Web page and linked to others.
- ♦ Audience-specific trades and media outlets (e.g., senior citizen publications).

E. See press release attached.

F. Timeline for release of materials

Charitable Gift Funds Strategy   February 1998   Local & Nat

Feb. 2-6	Approve release
Feb. 9-13	Develop press kits if necessary; develop database
Feb. 16-17	Mail or fax release to database
Feb. 18-20	Follow up by phone; resend material if needed
Feb. 23-27	Schedule interviews if necessary
March 2-4	Collect clips, write thank yous
March 5-6	Evaluate progress, initiate next steps

G. Potential Evaluation. The following is a sample of results compiled from this story release.

KDKA-TV2	35,000	Financial Show; 6 min. 2/22/98
WPXI-TV11	65,000	Financial Report 2/19/98
KDKA-AM	55,000	Tax savings advice 2/19/98 noon
KQV-News radio	50,000	Tax savings report 2/19/98 a.m. drive
WTAE-TV	75,000	Consumer alert 2/19/98
Chamber Newsletter	5,000	Strategies from our members section 2/20
Dynamic Business	5,500	Magazine for Small Business 3/98
Pittsburgh Business Times	19,000	Strategies section 3/2/98
Small Business News	26,000	Management Report 3/98
Tribune Review	250,000	Finance Section 2/22/98 Sunday
Penn Hills Progress	13,500	Neighbor to Watch section 2/25/98
Listed with Down Jones News Retrieval		
Listed with The Investor's Resource Wire		
Investment Advisor	(trade)	3/98
Financial Planning	(trade)	3/98
Smart Money Magazine	(trade)	3/98
The Wall Street Journal		2/23/98
Worth Magazine	(trade)	3/98

FOR IMMEDIATE RELEASE:
February 1998
CONTACT:
Thomas Smith, Innovative Financial Services at 413-777-8866

If You've Had a Good Year Financially
Charitable Gift Funds Could be For You

Pittsburgh, PA - Thomas Smith, ChFC, CLU, president of Innovative Financial Services, a downtown Pittsburgh financial planning firm, has helped clients achieve philanthropic goals while addressing tax and financial needs through the use of Charitable Gift Funds.

"If a client has experienced a peak income year, their contribution to the Gift Fund enables them to take a substantial tax deduction when they need it most, while at the same time allowing them to determine where and when the money will go to charities in future years," says Smith.

This approach can be particularly appealing to those individuals with a charitable inclination, but they still want to direct "who" gets the money. It's important to note that it's not just for wealthy people or people who have had recognizable financial success. It only takes $10,000 to start a Charitable Gift Fund. "It's a relatively new concept I predict will catch on very quickly as more people become aware of the benefits," says Smith.

For example, one of Smith's clients owned two related companies. The owner of the companies wanted to sell Company B to Company A. However, the sale would create a substantial income tax problem for the owner. Smith recommended an alternative to this tax burden, which also fell in line with the owner's ongoing desire to start a private foundation. Smith set up a Charitable Gift Fund, with many of the same attributes as a private foundation. By donating Company B's stock to the Charitable Gift Fund, the owner of the company was able to take a $270,000 tax deduction! Company A then purchased from the Gift Fund the stock in Company B for cash in the amount of $270,000. The Gift Fund was able to invest $270,000 and make future distributions as directed by the owner to the charities he preferred, all the while, the money was able to keep on growing each year tax-free. Finally, if the owner died, he could direct his children be given the authority to make future gifts. "The attractive part of this plan is there are no limits on the timeframe or the amount of money distributed," says Smith. "The client could recommend annual gifts to their church and community theater or favorite charity," he says.

There are many other ways to take advantage of the benefits of having a Charitable Gift Fund. For example, by donating low-cost basis stock to a Gift Fund, substantial capital gain taxes can be eliminated while receiving a deduction for the full, appraised value of the stock. In addition, many people make contributions to their Gift Fund on an annual basis to build endowments - particularly for alma maters. Families can set up a Charitable Gift Fund account rather than starting a private foundation in order to avoid the often prohibitive expense and administrative burdens of a private foundation. Smith sees opportunities to use Charitable Gift Funds in estate planning as well. ("By including a bequest to add to a Gift fund account, estate taxes can be reduced while the legacy of giving can be passed on to children and grandchildren," says Smith.)

A Charitable Gift Fund is easy to establish. The account can be opened with a donation of only $10,000 and subsequent contributions can be made in even smaller amounts. The initial gift to the Fund may be of cash or securities, including mutual fund shares and certain private or restricted stock. When ready, the Gift Fund will make recommended grants from your named account in amounts of $250 or more. The Fund provides all services related to the administration of the philanthropy and sends a letter with the grant check recognizing the donor as having recommended the gift (you can also remain anonymous). "My clients receive the pleasure of philanthropy without the responsibilities of management," says Smith.

There is a catch however. All donations to the charitable Gift Fund are irrevocable, so it is important to consider long-range plans and needs before choosing to give. "For the right client, it makes good business sense, plus it fulfills a deep personal commitment to charitable giving," says Smith.

Smith serves as an expert resource on topics such as asset allocation, money and asset management for affluent individuals/widows/divorcees, retirement planning, tax law changes and comprehensive financial planning. He is a Registered Principle for the National Association of Securities Dealers (NASD) and a Registered Investment Advisor. Thomas Smith has been in business for 27 years and has $120 million under management.

###

Appendix 2

....

A Public Relations Directory

The following is a list of sources that will help you compile an accurate and appropriate media list for your publicity efforts. Each of the directories in this section includes listings of media with name, address, and phone and fax numbers of the media contacts. In some cases, the information may also include circulation, frequency of publication, advertising rates, target audience, and other comments or remarks. Some of the directories are organized by subject matter and others by geographic location.

You will find many of these resources in the reference section of your local library. We've included phone numbers in case you are interested in purchasing the resource for your own personal library. Because such resources outdate themselves quickly, it's always wise to contact the particular medium to verify address and contact person before mailing anything out.

Publications

Chambers of commerce
Contact your local chamber for a local media list (radio, TV, print). Sometimes members receive the list at no cost; nonmembers for approximately $10 to $60.

Bacon's Publicity Checker   800-621-0561
Published annually, *Bacon's* lists magazines and newspapers in the U.S. and Canada in a two-volume set.

Burrelle's Media Directory   800-876-3342
Updated yearly, Burrelle's large volume covers media contacts for the U.S., Canada, and Mexico from newspapers, magazines, newsletters, radio, and television.

....

Editor and Publisher International Year Book 212-675-4380

Some call it the encyclopedia of the newspaper industry. It lists both U.S. and Canadian print media.. Every year *Editor & Publisher* magazine issues a special edition devoted to syndicates—it provides a directory of newspaper columnists. It can be purchased for $10 or as part of an annual subscription.

Gale Directory of Publications and Broadcast Media 800-877-GALE

In any local library, these large volumes list every publication and broadcast media in the nation by topic. You can also find these services provided on diskette, CD-rom, and online as well. Visit Gale's home page at http://www.gale.com.

National Directory of Newspaper Op-Ed Pages 800-331-8355

Op-Ed means "Opinion Editorial" submitted by readers of publications. The Op-Ed page is usually facing the editorial page, where the newspapers share their views on certain subjects. The Op-Ed page is usually a very popular page in a publication. You can also write to the publisher of this resource at Communication Creativity, Box 909-OF, Buena Vista, CO 81211.

Newsletter Clearinghouse 914-876-2081

Located on 44 West Market Street, P.O. Box 311, Rhinebeck, NY 12572, this organization is a good start if your PR campaign calls for corporate newsletters.

PR Newswire 800-832-5522

There are *Newswire* bureaus all over the country. For a fee, your press release will be sent to all media sources of your choice—locally, regionally, nationwide, and even internationally. You can visit the home page at http:www.prnewswire.com. It's excellent for obtaining late-breaking news.

Standard Rate and Data Service 773-256-6067

Standard Rate and Data Service (SRDS) publishes a host of monthly directories that may be helpful in developing a publicity plan. These include: *SRDS Newspapers Directory* and *SRDS Newspaper Rates and Data*; *SRDS Business Publication Rates and Data*, and; *SRDS Spot Television Rates and Data*, which lists TV stations in the U.S., Guam, and the Virgin Islands. Keep in mind the SRDS primarily provides advertising and marketing data.

Ulrich's International Periodicals Directory   **800-521-8110**

Great for information on magazines, especially foreign publications, *Ulrich's* lists publishers' names, editors' names and data on circulation and frequency of publication.

Writer's Market

Published by F&W Publications (1507 Dana Ave., Cincinnati, OH 45207), this resource is directed to writers to help them customize where and how to sell what they write. It's best for descriptions of magazines and trades throughout the U.S. It lists more than 4,000 places to sell articles, books, fillers, greeting cards, novels, plays, scripts, and short stories.

Clipping Services

For a fee, clipping services will search through newspapers and magazines nationwide for reference to your company, product, service, or industry and will "clip" and send your "hits" to you on a regular basis.

Bacon's Clipping Bureau	800-621-0561
Burrelle's Clipping Service and Media Information	800-631-1160
Mutual Press Clipping Services	215-569-4257
Luce Press Clippings, Inc.	212-889-6711

Public Relations Experts

O'Dwyer's Directory of Public Relations Firms   **212-679-2471**

This reference lists more than 1,400 individual firms and PR consultants in a variety of areas, including public relations, public affairs, investor relations, employee communications, corporate advertising, producer publicity, issues analysis, management forecasting, lobbying, proxy solicitation, TV speech training, and international PR.

Public Relations Society of America (PRSA)   **212-995-2230**

PRSA is the world's largest professional organization for public relations practitioners. With chapters all over the country, PRSA provides a forum for encouraging high standards of conduct as well as an exchange of information with other PR professionals. It's a place to start when you're searching for an answer to a question, a PR firm to help you with your publicity needs, or an intern to assist you. Headquartered at 33 Irving Place, New York, NY, 10003-2376.

Appendix 3

....

Sample Releases

Media releases—or press releases—generally follow the same format for any submission, whether for newspapers, magazines, TV, or radio.

- ♦ A banner head identifies what type of release it is. For example: "News Release," "Calendar Release," or "Public Service Announcement."

- ♦ The date and contact name, title, organization, and phone number of the contact should always be in the top right-hand or left-hand corner—easy to find in a quick glance.

- ♦ The headline generally is a brief, active statement in capital letters and centered on the page under the contact information.

- ♦ The dateline appears before the beginning of the first paragraph of the text—also called the lead. This includes the city, state, and date of the release.

- ♦ If the release runs onto more than one page, make sure the pages are numbered.

- ♦ On all subsequent pages, a small descriptive header should be included in the top left-hand corner; including a short description, page number and total number of pages. For example: "Mr. Smith wins award—page 2 of 2."

In this appendix, several sample releases are included for you to study and familiarize yourself with the format.

NEWS RELEASE

FOR IMMEDIATE RELEASE
November 30, 1997

CONTACT:
Judy Smith
VP of Public Relations
Arc Communications
523-666-6666

**MATTHEW NOBLES TO HEAD DALLAS-BASED ELECTRONICS DIVISION
FOR ARC COMMUNICATIONS**

Dallas, TX (11-30-97) - Matthew Nobles, 34, has been named President and Chief
Executive Officer of Arc Communications' Electronics Division. It was announced today
by the Philadelphia-based firm.

Nobles had been the vice president of electronics for Lacon Electronics, a leading
manufacturer of voice-activated computer equipment. Nobles has been credited by Acon
for increasing the number of United States outlets by 35% and helping the company
expand into the European markets.

Nobles' role at Arc will be to increase revenues by accelerating Arc's key
products into overseas markets. He is expected to consolidate several of Arc's
manufacturing facilities. He is also expected to build a second headquarters in Paris,
France.

Prior to joining Lacon in 1988, Nobles was the General Manager for MotionWare,
a manufacturer of motion sensors for electronic doors found in hospital emergency rooms
across the nation. A 1985 graduate of Villanova University, his first position out of

(more)

college was with IBM in Philadelphia.

Arc Communications is known for revolutionary "talking computers" used mainly by line staff of major manufacturers to increase speed of work flow, document key information and provide an archive of data that can be explored for efficiencies. Their most popular product on the market today is called, "Talk Hero" and is used by leading companies including the Ford Motor Company.

###

NEWS RELEASE

FOR IMMEDIATE RELEASE
October 1, 1996

CONTACT:
Hank Walshak
The Pennsylvania Speakers Association
412-456-2121

MYSTERY ENTERTAINER COMES TO PENNSYLVANIA SPEAKERS ASSOCIATION ON SATURDAY, DECEMBER 14

South Hills, PA - On Saturday, December 14, 1996, the Pennsylvania Speakers Association welcomes Mystery Entertainer, Craig Karges, 38, to the Green Tree Marriott Hotel from noon to 5 p.m. for his acclaimed program, "Experience the Extraordinary." Cost is $25 for members and $40 for non-members.

A table "walks" on stage and then flies into the air! Borrowed finger rings from the members are linked together in chain. Thoughts are read, predictions are made and verified by **Craig Karges, extraordinist**. His unusual blend of mystery, humor, psychology, magic, psychic and intuition will dazzle the mind as he challenges his audiences to question what is real and unreal, what is possible and impossible. You don't just watch this performance, you experience it, through total audience participation. The goal is to help participants test their intuition, learn memory techniques, and tap into their subconscious to enhance their creativity and decision making skills. Overall, the show is geared toward participants experiencing greater personal power and to achieve success more easily.

(more)

Karges says he does not possess supernatural powers, nor does he claim to perform as a psychic or a magician. While he acknowledges that he is an entertainer, and showmanship plays a role in what he does, he insists that he does not prearrange anything with members of the audience. Skeptical? He has a standing offer of $25,000, payable to charity if anyone can prove he uses "plants" from the audience to accomplish his demonstrations!

"The idea is to put you in awe of your own mind," says Karges. "Once you experience the extraordinary, you will rethink your own definition of what is really possible in terms of achieving success, not just in business, but in your daily life as well." Karges continues, "Ordinary people are capable of achieving extraordinary results," says Karges. "My performance reveals how to grow and create lasting change in your life by learning to effectively utilize the extraordinary abilities of your mind."

Karges began his career as an entertainer, specializing in appearances on college and university campuses. His success in this field was so overwhelming that the national Association for Campus Activities named him Campus Entertainer of the Year, an award previously held by rock stars like Huey Lewis and the News and the Police. From the college circuit, Craig turned his attention to the corporate industry. he has presented for corporate giants like IBM, General Motors and General Electric. He has given over 2,000 presentations in 49 states and Canada. In addition to live performances, his book has sold in 11 countries; he has co-produced and starred in two half hour television specials for PBS in his home state of West Virginia; and he

(more)

Page 3 - Mystery Entertainer, PA Speakers Association

has appeared on numerous national television shows and cable specials. Performance magazine called the 38-year old extraordinist's presentation, "the next era in mystery entertainment." Jay Leno of the Tonight Show says, "he's a huge hit!" The Chicago Tribune called his presentation, "an uplifting experience - what he does is magical." HBO Talk Show Host, Dennis Miller puts it this way, "this wierds me out." The Pennsylvania Speakers Association, a non-profit chapter of the National Speakers Association is an organization designed for "anyone who speaks" either personally or professionally to learn how to effectively deliver messages to an audience.

Call 412-456-2121 to make reservations for this unprecedented event.

###

CALENDAR ANNOUNCEMENT

FOR IMMEDIATE RELEASE:
October, 3, 1997

CONTACT:
Tom Reda, TSBN at 412-487-0303

SPEAKER TO EDUCATE SMALL BUSINESS PROFESSIONALS ON THE 12 MISTAKES TO AVOID WHEN HIRING AT MEETING OF THE SMALL BUSINESS NETWORK

McCandless Township, PA - On Wednesday, November 19, 1997 from 6 to 9 p.m. at the

Wildwood Country Club in the North Hills, The Small Business Network (TSBN) will

hold its monthly meeting featuring a popular topic for small business owners, "The 12

Mistakes to Avoid When Hiring." The speaker will be Tom Reda, owner of TSBN.

Dinner will be provided, therefore R.S.V.P.'s are required. Call 412-487-0303 to register,

and for more information.

###

FORMAT #2:

CALENDAR ANNOUNCEMENT
(date you're sending the release)

Note: Please list the following in your calendar of events. Thank you.

ORGANIZATION:	The Small Business Network (TSBN)
CONTACT NAME AND NUMBER:	Tom Reda at 412-487-0303
LOCATION:	Wildwood Country Club, North Hills
DATE AND TIME OF EVENT:	November 19, 1997 from 6-9 p.m.
TOPIC:	The 12 Mistakes to Avoid When Hiring
KEYNOTE SPEAKER:	Tom Reda, president of TSBN
IMPORTANT INFORMATION:	TSBN is an organization dedicated to the education and sharing of ideas amongst successful small business owners.

-30- OR ### (indicates the end)

NEWS RELEASE

FOR IMMEDIATE RELEASE:
June 4, 1996

CONTACT:
Janet Lerchey at Acme Enterprises
214-368-2178

BUSINESSWOMAN RECEIVES SECOND AWARD

Portland, OR (6-4-96)- The recipient of the National Athena Award for outstanding woman in business, Janet Lerchey, president of Acme Enterprises, has also been recognized by the Pennsylvania Department of Commerce and the Governor's Commission for Women in association with the Business Journals of Pennsylvania as one of the Top 50 Women in Business in the State of Pennsylvania. Lerchey is an expert in "remote access," enabling professionals to work from remote sites, primarily their homes, to increase productivity and enhance flexibility in the workplace.

###

NEWS RELEASE

FOR IMMEDIATE RELEASE:
January 21, 1998

CONTACT:
Cronin Communications at 412-366-2187

MERGE TO FORM THE LARGEST PRIVATE ORTHOPAEDIC PRACTICE IN GREATER PITTSBURGH

Pittsburgh, PA - Oakland Orthopaedic Associates and MH&D Orthopedic Associates, Inc., two orthopaedic groups with offices in the Greater Pittsburgh area, have agreed to merge to form Greater Pittsburgh Orthopaedic Associates (GPOA). The move, effective March 1, 1998, will make GPOA the largest private orthopaedic practice in the Greater Pittsburgh region.

Physicians representing all orthopaedic specialties for GPOA will include: M. Russell Leslie, M.D., Ronald G. Mehok, M.D., Heywood A. Haser, M.D., James A. D'Antonio, M.D., V. Thomas Worrall, M.D., Jonathan E. Hottenstein, M.D., Michael D. Miller, M.D., Gary L. Smith, M.D., Michael P. Casey, M.D., Michael W. Bowman, M.D., James P. Bradley, M.D., Jon A. Levy, M.D., Michael J. Rytel, M.D., and Jeffrey B. Mulholland, M.D.

Offices will be located in Moon Township, Pittsburgh, Brackenridge, Sewickley, Cranberry and Avalon, PA. GPOA's group physicians have privileges with Allegheny General Hospital, Allegheny Valley Hospital, Citizens General Hospital, Sewickley

(more)

Merge forms largest practice - page 2 of 2

Valley Hospital, St. Francis Medical Center, St. Francis Surgery Center North, Suburban General Hospital, University of Pittsburgh Medical Center (UPMC), UPMC Beaver Valley, UPMC Passavant, UPMC Shadyside, and UPMC St. Margaret.

To facilitate the merger, GPOA has welcomed Michael L. Sandnes, 42, an executive from Miami, FL to serve as Chief Executive Officer. "Our future plans are to expand on a regional scale and become a major center of excellence as a quality provider of comprehensive orthopaedic care." Linda Fleming, CPA, 43, who has served as Executive Director for Oakland Orthopaedic Associates for 17 years, has been appointed to serve as Chief Financial Officer.

GPOA specialties include arthroscopy, arthritis surgery, foot, knee and ankle surgery, general orthopaedics, hand and elbow surgery, shoulder surgery, shoulder surgery, spine surgery, sports medicine, total joint replacement.

###

NEWS RELEASE

FOR IMMEDIATE RELEASE:
August 13, 1995
CONTACT:
Robert V. Capalbo at 412-372-4608

A FUTURE WITHOUT FILM?

Capalbo Studios offers "instant results" with filmless Digital Photography

Pitcairn, PA - He saw it coming...and he took the leap...into the world of Digital

Photography, that is. Imagine high resolution images that rival the costliest of film

work or on-screen previewing plus image and art enhancement. Wouldn't it be ideal

to have one system shoot images, then retouch great shots into perfect shots, separate

the colors perfectly for printing and of course, get a print within two minutes? (It's

finally here in Pittsburgh, thanks to Robert V. Capalbo's leap of faith.)

About 5 years ago, Robert V. Capalbo had a hunch that the future of photography was

going to be digital and that conventional methods were eventually going to be too

slow, too cumbersome and perhaps lacking quality and adding expense. After doing

some homework, Capalbo made a significant investment in the T2 Filmless Digital

Back - one of the few independent studios this side of the Mississippi to have one - to

play a revolutionary role in commercial photography for the significant cost savings,

time savings and versatility in application it offers the creative industry as opposed to

traditional photography. The hunch paid off.

(more)

Digital Photography - page 2

"It's the cutting edge of technology offering our clients high quality digital images and limitless creative effects," says Capalbo. "This system is unbelievable. The future of photography is here today!"

Robert V. Capalbo Photography is currently offering digital photography to its customer base which includes many (downtown Pittsburgh) advertising agencies such as Hallmark Tassone, Blattner Brunner as well as corporate clients such as Giant Eagle, GNC, National Record Mart, Pittsburgh Brewing Company. Many of his customers say they would never go back to the "traditional" method of shooting film. "My clients have been spoiled by this capture station," says Capalbo.

You have to see it to believe it. Mounted on a conventional 4x5 camera, the T2 effortlessly converts the image you would normally see through a conventional camera into a high resolution digital image which displays on an integrated video monitor. As a result, you do not just see a Polaroid, you see the actual finished shot without having to wait for expensive and time-consuming lab work.

From a printing standpoint, digital photography saves a significant amount of money because the separation phase of print production is completely eliminated. High quality digital color separations are executed through proprietary software that can adapt to any printer specification. The system offers high end retouching for even the most complicated image. With the T2, the image intensity, contrast and color

(more)

Digital Photography - page 3

saturation can be fine tuned on the screen as soon as the image is captured. Using state of the art computer tools, the image can be dodged, ghosted, blended or retouched to perfection.

For art directors, it saves time, for they are able to view the finished image on the computer screen and make changes if necessary. They can leave either with prints or with the image on disk ready to be placed into any page layout or format of their choice which in turn eliminates the negative stripping phase. For location shooting, Capalbo is able to travel around the country with his staff and portable digital equipment to ensure accuracy and quality.

To maintain his role as a leader in the digital industry, Capalbo has also invested in a digital printer to complement his digital system. The printer, the Fujix Pictrography 3000, is the only one of its kind that prints on photosensitive paper in 2 minutes or less. It has been rated as the best in its class for reproduction quality continuous tone prints. "This is a must-have tool for the creative industry when clean, clear, reproduction-quality digital prints are needed yesterday," says Capalbo.

The results of this investment speak for itself. A small business can now easily compete with big business because of the quality of technology. Capalbo is available when his schedule permits for demonstrations either in studio or on location. He travels for professional speaking engagements and provides consulting services to companies nationwide.

###

PUBLIC SERVICE ANNOUNCEMENT

FOR IMMEDIATE RELEASE
<<date>>
CONTACT:
The Girl Scouts of Southwestern Pennsylvania
Barbara Bettwy at 1-800-248-3355

GIRL SCOUTS TO HOST THE FIRST ANNUAL WOMEN OF DISTINCTION AWARDS

:30 JOIN THE GIRL SCOUTS OF SOUTHWESTERN PENNSYLVANIA ON SEPTEMBER 23, 1997 AT 5:15 P.M. AT THE WESTIN WILLIAM PENN FOR THE FIRST ANNUAL WOMEN OF DISTINCTION AWARDS. THE GIRL SCOUTS WILL HONOR WOMEN YOU KNOW IN BUSINESS, COMMUNITY SERVICE AND SERVICE TO GIRL SCOUTING. IT'S ONLY FIFTEEN DOLLARS AND THE MONEY GOES TO A GOOD CAUSE. CALL THE GIRL SCOUTS AT 1-800-248-3355 TO RESERVE YOUR SEAT!

-30-

Appendix 4

Sample Media Kit

The following is a sample of a complete media kit including:

♦ Press Release

♦ Fact Sheet

♦ Backgrounder

♦ Quote Sheet

♦ Clip Sheet

This media kit was compiled to announce the plans for a new building, the North Shore Business Center. You can find more detailed descriptions of these tools in Chapter 7. This particular press kit is comprehensive and also includes (but not appearing in this book) financial information for the Center, a map of the site for the Center, a reprint of an article about the organization, photos of key people, and a brochure about the nonprofit organization. The information was placed in a plain, white, pocket folder with a sticker of the logo on the front. It is simple, rather inexpensive and very effective.

NorthSide

civic development council inc

NEWS RELEASE

FOR IMMEDIATE RELEASE
July 1, 1997

CONTACT:
Emily Buka, NSCDC
412-333-3333

NORTH SIDE CIVIC DEVELOPMENT COUNCIL
REVEALS PLANS FOR NORTH SHORE BUSINESS CENTER
ON JULY 30 AT RIVERSIDE COMMONS CELEBRATION

North Side Pittsburgh, PA (7-30-97) - At 10 a.m. on Wednesday, July 30, 1997 at Riverside Commons, 700 River Avenue, The North Side Civic Development Council (NSCDC) will reveal plans and drawings for the North Shore Business Center, an inner-city industrial office park located on the North Shore of Pittsburgh.

This multi-use development will be supervised by Riverfront Development Partners, a collaboration between the Bidwell Cultural and Training Center and the North Side Industrial Development Company (NSIDC), the real estate development affiliate of the community-based North Side Civic Development Council, to develop high-quality, mixed-use space in a prime location to attract companies which will provide jobs and training for community residents; create an inner-city location for light manufacturing; revitalize the urban landscape; and beautify the city's riverfront.

The unveiling will be part of the 5th Anniversary Celebration for Riverside Commons, a $7.5 million incubator renovation facility located in a state Enterprise Zone housing new small businesses, particularly women and minority-owned firms.

civic development council inc

"Since Riverside Commons is currently at 100% capacity housing 38 small businesses and employing 250 people, "graduates" will be relocated to the North Shore Business Center, which is adjacent to Riverside Commons," says Emily Buka, president of NSCDC. Since its inception, more than 400 jobs have been created representing 50 companies.

"The North Shore Business Center is one more major step to achieving the Council's mission - to increase economic activity and employment in the North Side," says Buka, who will present the plans for the North Shore Business Center to city, county, state officials as well as more than 100 business and community leaders scheduled to attend. "We serve as a unique catalyst for urban revitalization by advising, participating in and supporting commercial and residential projects," Buka says. Buka was recently selected as a finalist for the prestigious 1997 Entrepreneur of the Year Awards as Supporter of Entrepreneurship for her efforts.

For example, in addition to the North Shore Business Center and Riverside Commons, NSCDC has developed 250,000 sq. ft. of commercial space in several locations in the North Side and has obtained $7 million in Pennsylvania Industrial Development Authority (PIDA) loans from the Commonwealth for new and existing ventures, enabling it to provide commercial space, technical assistance and business support to approximately 250 new and existing businesses and assisting in the creation of 1,600 new jobs.

NorthSide

civic development council inc

The unveiling of the North Shore Business Center is part of a day-long

EXPO. In addition to the unveiling at 10 a.m., highlights of the day include:

8:30 a.m.   Partnership Breakfast, Riverside Commons Conference Room

The purpose of this event is to celebrate the accomplishments of Riverside Commons

and the upcoming North Shore Business Center. Neighboring corporations,

institutions, community based organizations and dignitaries will have the opportunity

to learn more about the mission and work of the North Side Civic Development

Council. Invited guests include corporate, business, civic, and banking leaders. Hosts

will include city, county and state elected officials including State Representatives

Don Walko and Bill Robinson. Remarks will be made by Attorney Martha Helmreich,

NSCDC Board Chair, Emily Buka, President of NSCDC and members of the Host

Committee.

10 a.m. - 10:30 a.m. ***UNVEILING OF THE NORTH SHORE BUSINESS

CENTER - Riverside Commons PHOTO OPPORTUNITY

10:30 - 10:45 a.m.   Ribbon Cutting for Riverside Commons EXPO

10:45-12:00 p.m.   Riverside Commons Tour and EXPO

Tours conducted by Staff and Board Members

12:00 to 2:00 p.m.   Luncheon, Bidwell Training Center, 1815 Metropolitan

Street, North Side

At noon, the celebration will move from Riverside Commons to the Bidwell Training

Center for a luncheon featuring keynote speaker, Derrick Span, director of the Project

for Community Building, Department of Community and Economic Development,

civic development council inc

who will present "The Project for Community Building," a new $19 million state initiative establishing community development banks, savings accounts for the working poor, a self-employment program for the unemployed and community crime prevention grants. According to Governor Tom Ridge who appointed Span to direct the ambitious initiative based on "his professional experience in building communities and bringing them together," the Project is designed to spearhead efforts to urge government agencies at state and local levels to launch collaborative endeavors. Span, 39, is a former radio and TV host, newspaper columnist, college professor and former president of the Urban League of Harrisburg. Alfonso Jackson, Minority Business Development Authority, Claire Morrison, Department of Public Welfare, and Bridget Des Ogugua, director of Minority Business Development Authority, will offer remarks. State Senators Jack Wagner and Leonard Bodack are members of the host committee.

2:00 - 3:00 p.m.	**Special Business Forum with Derrick Span, Bidwell Training Center Library - PHOTO OPPORTUNITY.**
3:00 - 6:00 p.m.	**Jazz Combo and Picnic, Riverside Commons Grounds**
3:00 - 6:00 p.m.	**Riverside Commons Facility Tours and EXPO**

NORTH SIDE CIVIC DEVELOPMENT COUNCIL PROVIDES COMMUNITY AND ECONOMIC DEVELOPMENT SERVICES

The North Side Civic Development Council provides business development services including loan packaging, marketing, planning and technical support for entrepreneurs, and it works to attract outside businesses to the region, assisting in site

civic development council inc

selection, as well as to create businesses, many minority and women-owned. "North Side's Own" is one of the most notable recent projects of the organization.

North Side's Own is a new, employee-owned company of home-based, low income women of the North Side who use state-of-the-art sewing technology to create high quality merchandise including clothing and textile product manufacturing. More than 100 jobs have been created for disadvantaged workers formerly unemployed, on welfare or in low-paying jobs. The project is directed by Jackie Hill, vice president of NSCDC.

###

NorthSide

civic development council inc

North Side Civic Development Council, Inc.
North Shore Business Center
FACT SHEET

Executive Summary

The North Shore Business Center is a multi-use development to be undertaken by Riverfront Development Partners, a collaboration of SPEDD, BIDCO and the North Side Industrial Development Company (NSIDC). The initial phases of the project will be located on a site adjacent to Riverside Commons Innovation Center, the small business incubator developed by the NSIDC and BIDCO and managed by SPEDD. Predevelopment funds of $175,000 will be used to pay for architectural, engineering and environmental studies as well as options to purchase the five privately held parcels.

Preliminary Start-Up Cost Estimates

Options-One Year	$100,000
Environmental-Phase I	15,000
Surveys and Soils Tests	15,000
Legal and Title	15,000
Architectural	15,000
Developers Fee	15,000
Total	$175,000

The Players

The North Shore Business Center is the brainchild of a team which includes specialists in business development, job training and community redevelopment. SPEDD, BIDCO, subsidiary of the Bidwell Training Center, and the North Side Industrial Development Company (NSIDC), the real estate development affiliate of the community-based North Side Civic Development Council, have formed a partnership, Riverfront Development Partners.

Mission

Our mission is the development of high-quality, mixed-use space in a prime location with the purpose of 1) attracting companies, which will maximize employment and training opportunities for community residents, 2) creating an inner-city location for light manufacturing, 3) revitalizing the urban landscape, and 4) beautifying the City's riverfront.

NorthSide

civic development council inc

North Side Civic Development Council, Inc.
North Shore Business Center
FACT SHEET

The Site
The site for the North Shore Business Center has some of the most attractive features of any inner-city or suburban location. First, the total site from the Railroad bridge to the Heinz Plant is self-contained. The physical and topographic barriers, including the Expressway and the River, will facilitate site control and help to prevent adjacent uses, which would negatively affect the project. Plus the site is small enough to accommodate a controllable amount of development. The larger site is split in half by the columns supporting the Veterans Bridge, which facilitates phasing of the development at least into two parts. Parking available under the bridge is one of the most beneficial features of the location.

The Timeline

January -May 1995	Securing predevelopment funds
May-October 1995	Acquiring options to purchase various properties
November-June 1995	Negotiating financing with PA Industrial Development Authority (PIDA)
July-December 1996	Construction of Phase I
January 1997-June 1998	Leasing of Phase I building, depending on progress of leasing of Phase II

Anticipated Results
The North Shore Business Park is an exceptional opportunity to develop space which is flexible and easily adaptable to the multi-faceted needs of contemporary businesses. The expected outcomes of the project are:

- Attraction of companies, hopefully, from outside the region to the inner city
- Serving a previously untapped market niche by providing flex space
- Job creation by providing non-existent flex space in the inner city
- Job training and placement, assisted by Bidwell, to be promoted via the project's leasing and marketing program
- Remediation of possible environmental damage
- Continued beautification and public access to the riverfront in keeping with the city's public policy and adding value to the heritage Trail
- Increase in the City's tax base

NorthSide

civic development council inc

Biography
Emily Buka, President
North Side Civic Development Council, Inc.

Emily Buka is currently the President of the North Side Civic Development Council, responsible for the community development of one-third of the city of Pittsburgh's land mass and over 60,000 people. In that capacity, she orchestrates the economic development initiatives of one of the most important community development corporations in Pittsburgh. Included in the Council's real estate portfolio is Riverside Commons Innovation Center, a 50,000 sq. ft. incubator targeted to start-up companies, primarily women and minority-owned businesses. Emily has successfully completed the construction including tenant build-out and leased the property to 100%. As a small business incubator development, Emily also administers the business support program, including the shared office services as well as direct hands-on assistance to Riverside's 44 incubator tenants.

Prior to joining the Civic Council in 1992, Emily spent three years working with financial institutions in the work-out of their non-performing real estate assets. In 1989, she joined the Grant Street National Bank in Liquidation, a creation of Mellon Bank to dispose of properties and loans. After liquidating over a $75 million portfolio which projects ranged from office building to time-share resorts, Emily joined Westinghouse Credit Corporation to work out similar problem properties, including a $117 million shopping center and $32 million hotel.

Emily's experience in the field of real estate work out was a natural progression from her previous ten years as a real estate developer. With Mellon Stuart Realty, Emily was personally responsible for the development of a 100,000 sq. ft. medical office building in the heart of the University of Pittsburgh Medical Center and directed the construction and leasing of Commerce Court at Station Square.

Emily is a graduate of Chatham College and received a degree in Urban and Regional Planning from the University of Pittsburgh in 1978. She has completed advanced real estate development courses at Harvard, NYU and the Wharton School. She has served on the Pine Township Planning Commission, been a member of Building Owners and Managers Association and Women in Real Estate as well as served as the past president of the local chapter of the National Association of Industrial and Office Parks. She is currently a Director of the Metropolitan Board of the YMCA.

Emily lives in Chatham Village, Mount Washington and has two children, Stephanie and Adrienne.

NorthSide

civic development council inc

North Side Civic Development Council, Inc.
North Shore Business Center
Quote Sheet

Martha Helmreich, esq.   NSCDC Board Chair
"One of the most positive outcomes of the development of the concept of the North Shore Business Center was the experience of working as a team, meshing our expertise, and developing mutual goals for success."

Derrick Span   Director of the Project for Community Building,
Department of Community and Economic Development
State of Pennsylvania
"The North Side Civic Development Council serves as a positive example to spearhead efforts to urge other agencies at state and local levels to launch collaborative endeavors for community development."

Alfonso Jackson   Minority Business Development Authority
"The North Shore Business Center is a catalyst for minorities and women owned companies to make their mark in the private business sector. "

Claire Morrison   Department of Public Welfare
"There are individuals making a difference, a big difference at the North Side Civic Development Council. They should be commended for not only speaking their mission, but acting upon it."

Bridget Des Ogugua   Director of Minority Business Development Authority
State of Pennsylvania
"The power in the North Shore Business Center lies not only in the building but it's programming which will promote job creation and training. Successful collaboration with companies like American Express and Miles Laboratories, where training is provided for specific services, allows companies to take advantage of these non-mandatory programs and help to create a skilled work force."

NorthSide

civic development council inc

SUCCESSFUL TRAINING PROGRAM FOR NORTH SIDE WORKING MOTHERS LEADS TO NEW JOBS AND SMALL BUSINESS OWNERSHIP

PROGRAM WAS HIGHLIGHTED AT THE NORTH SIDE CIVIC DEVELOPMENT COUNCIL'S RIVERSIDE COMMONS CELEBRATION ON JULY 30

A group of hard-working mothers from the North Side of Pittsburgh are busy "sewing up the details" - literally - of their dream to create more jobs and a thriving business enterprise, manufacturing and selling children's clothing and textile products. This cooperative enterprise known as "North Side's Own" is the brainchild of the North Side Civic Development Council, Inc., led by Jacqueline Hill, vice president. "Our goal is to create an alternative to public assistance, unemployment and low paying service jobs," says Hill.

By utilizing state of the art sewing technology in home-based sewing centers, 75 North Side's Own participants, who are also owners of the enterprise, will create smaller quantities of high quality children's clothing . A variety of simply designed textile products will also be produced under contract for designers and merchandisers. Finished goods will be brought to a central plant location on commercial property currently owned by the North Side Civic Development Council, Inc., where an another estimated 25 participants will handle order shipping, quality control inspection and other tasks such as pressing, packaging, etc.

"Within three to five years, North Side's Own will create employment and business ownership opportunities for 100 low-income individuals," explains Hill. Currently, participants meet every Wednesday and Friday at 10 a.m. on the North Side.

NorthSide

civic development council inc

In fact, Hill explains that the structure of North Side's Own allows them to offer children's clothing retailers a better profit margin on their own private labels than what they currently receive on popular brands.

"The core of North Side's Own is for participants to contribute to the profitability of their enterprise while still engaged in the advanced portions of the training process," says Hill. The project will provide the skills, knowledge and capital required to start and operate the textile manufacturing business. In addition, participants will encounter three distinct training modules to include 1) sewing skills - to create finished goods on high-tech sewing equipment; 2) self-development - including time management, conflict resolution, communication, problem solving and team building skills; 3) business training - offering finance, management and operation skills.

Participants who have successfully completed the three training modules will have the opportunity to purchase their own sewing centers including a sewing machine, shelved cabinet, allowing for a secluded work space within the home. "A loan fund will be established to assist the participants in this expenditure of approximately $1500," says Hill.

Hill continues, "Our big dream is to carefully expand our product line to include children's clothing under the North Side's Own label and develop specialty products such as Afro-Centric clothing and stylish clothing for the handicapped and elderly."

Hill says that North Side's Own benefits from extensive community support in the form of a strong and active Community Advisory Board, multiple partnerships with other community organizations and access to a wealth of technical assistance from various local business support centers and universities.

civic development council inc

The North Side Civic Development Council, Inc.'s mission is to increase economic activity in Pittsburgh, particularly on the North Side by attracting new businesses and creating new businesses in the area. North Side Civic is best known for the development of Riverside Commons, a small business incubator on the North Shore of Pittsburgh, now leasing more than 40 small, thriving businesses and the North Shore Business Center. In addition, this non-profit organization, served by 18 board members who are prominent members of the North Side business community, recently helped Reinhold Ice Cream expand into the area, assisting with loan packaging for a new plant site which resulted in many new jobs. In addition to loan packaging, North Side Civic also assists companies and individuals on or near the North Side of Pittsburgh with marketing advice, technical support and business planning information.

North Side Civic Development Council, Inc. accepts donations from businesses and individuals committed to increasing economic activity for the North Side community and ultimately Pittsburgh, PA . For more information, contact Jacqueline Hill or Emily Buka at 412-322-3523.

###

....

Guidelines for Photos; Photo Release Form

A picture is worth a thousand words

A picture with a caption describing it may be worth more to you than a large publicity story. Why? Think about the way you read a newspaper or magazine. Your eye is automatically attracted to the photos first. Photos pique curiosity, they are usually the first things that are viewed on a page and they leave an indelible impression on the mind. The best thing you can shoot for is a photo *and* a story!

Mechanics for submitting photos

1. Generally, submit glossy, 8 x 10 color or black and white photos unless the newspaper has a different size preference. Use 5 x 7 head and shoulders shots to accompany announcements about individuals.

2. Always label the back of the photo using a felt-tip marker. Include name, organization, title, address, and phone. Never use a pen or pencil as it damages the photo for reproduction purposes.

3. The photo must be top quality as technology is changing even as you read this sentence. According to *The New York Times*, more than 97 percent of North American newspapers print some of their pages in color. When you revise your media list periodically, request information about the use of black and white photos.

4. The caption can be typed and adhered to the back of the photo, if it is brief. If not, type the caption on the lower portion of a white sheet of paper and tape the caption to the back of the photo so the photo editor can study the photo and the caption simultaneously.

....

5. If you're mailing the photo, put the photo and the caption between two pieces of cardboard so the photo doesn't bend or get smudged, and write "photo enclosed, do not bend" on the other portion of your mailing envelope.

6. Never use paper clips or staples with your photos. Do not type directly on the back of the photo. Instead type on a label and adhere it to the photo.

7. Most daily papers have their own photo staff. But if you are submitting photos by a photographer who wants credit, most publications will include a "credit line" with these photos. Typically, this credit line will run along one of the borders of the photo in small type. When you submit such photos, be sure to indicate which ones require a credit line, offering the exact language. For example: "Photo by Stephen J. Thomas Studios."

The unwritten rules

◆ The photo desk is very busy. Try not to call unless it is absolutely necessary.

◆ Don't expect a photo to be returned and, by all means, do not call and ask for it.

◆ Make sure the publication you're submitting to accepts photos. Many only send their own photographers. If a photographer is assigned to shoot the photo, do not request prints for your own use, unless you know the newspaper has a policy that allows you to purchase them.

When to use photo release forms

There may be a rare time when you must provide a newspaper with a signed photo release form. Or you may want a release because you plan to use the photo again for various applications. Make sure you obtain a release if you have hired a model for a shot or have included a child in a photo. A sample photo release form follows. Keep the original signature with your files and attach a copy of the release form to the original photo.

Photo Release Form

I, _____(subject's name), being of legal age, hereby consent and authorize _____ (organization's name), its successors, legal representative and assigns, to use and reproduce my name and photograph(s) or the name and photograph(s) of _____(name of minor and relationship), taken by _____(photographer) on _____(date), and circulate the same for any and all purposes, including public information of every description.

_____(signature)

_____(address)

Appendix 6

Books Worth Reading

The Business of Special Events. Freedman, Harry A & Feldman, Karen. Pineapple Press, 1997.

Communicating When Your Company is Under Siege. Pindsdorf, Marion K. Fordham University Press, 1997.

Confessions of a PR Man. Wood, Robert J. (with Max Gunther). NAL Penguin Inc., 1988.

Crisis Response: Inside Stories on Managing Image Under Siege. Gottshalk, Jack A. Visible Ink Press, 1993.

The Discipline of Market Leaders: Choose Your Customers, Narrow Your Focus, Dominate Your Market. Treacy, Michael & Wiersema, Fred. Addison Wesley, 1995.

Essentials of Media Planning. Barban, Cristol, Kopec. NTC Business Books. 800-323-4900, 1994.

Expose Yourself: Using the Power of Public Relations to Promote your Business and Yourself. Beals, Melba. Chronicle Books, 1990.

"Generating All the Free Publicity You'll Ever Need" (Special Report). Gage, Randy. Florida: Gage Research & Development Institute, Inc. 800-432-GAGE, 1995.

Guerrilla Marketing. Levinson, Jay Conrad. New York: Houghton Mifflin, 1993.

Guerrilla P.R.: How you can Wage an Effective Publicity Campaign Without Going Broke. Levine, Michael. Harper Collins, 1993.

A Guide to Preparing Cost-effective Press Releases. Loeffler, Robert H. Haworth Marketing and Resources, 1993.

How to Promote, Publicize and Advertise Your Growing Business: Getting the Word Out Without Spending a Fortune. Baker, Sunny & Kim. Wiley, 1989.

The Marketing Sourcebook for Small Business. Davidson, Jeffrey. Wiley, 1989.

The New Publicity Kit: A Complete Guide for Entrepreneurs, Small Businesses & Nonprofit Organizations. Smith, Jeanette. Wiley, 1996.

Persuading on Paper. Yudkin, Marcia. Penguin Books, 1996.

The Persuasion Explosion: Your Guide to the Power and Influence of Contemporary Public Relations. Stevens, Art. Acropolis Books, 1985.

Power and Influence: Mastering the Art of Persuasion. Dilenschneider, Robert L. Prentice Hall, 1990.

Power PR: A Streetfighters Handbook to Winning Public Relations. Hill, Dennis Cole. Lifetime Books, 1990.

Publicity and Public Relations. Doty, Dorothy I. Barron's Educational Series, 1990.

Six Steps to Free Publicity. Yudkin, Marcia. Penguin Books, 1994.

Soundbites: A Business Guide for Working with the Media. Kerchner, Kathy. Savage Press, 1997.

Targeted Public Relations: How to Get Thousands of Dollars of Free Publicity for Your Product, Service Organization or Idea. Bly, Robert W. Henry Holt, 1994.

The Unabashed Self-Promoter's Guide: What Every Man, Woman, and Child Needs to Know About Getting Ahead by Exploiting the Media. Lant, Jeffrey. NLA, 1996.

You Can Hype Anything. Pinsky, Raleigh. Carol Publishing Group, NY, 1995.

....

Internet Sites Worth Visiting

ABC News

www.abcnews.com

Has a slideshow of photos on current events.

Bacon's Media Directory

www.baconsinfo.com

Books on Publicity

www.amazon.com

www.orion.org/library/sgcl/bookmore/bl-pr.html

www.cifrd.org.tw/patnckc/prfile/prebook.html

Note: Amazon offers an online service where they will "watch" for books on the subject of your choice.

Burrelle's Media Directory

www.asog.co.at/SPCatoalo/bmdr.html

Cronin Communications

www.cyberscoreinc.com/cronin

Send an e-mail from this Web site to receive free information on how to cash in on thousands of dollars of free publicity!

Directories

www.prsa.org/greenbl/director.html

Lists media information particularly from Europe and New York City.

....

Editor & Publisher International Year Book
www.mediainfo.com

Gale Directory of Broadcast Media
www.gale.com

Luce Press Clipping Service
www.lucepress.com

Mailing Lists
www.liszt.com

Professional Associations
www.westwords.com/Guffey/assoc.html

PR Newswire
www.prnewswire.com

Publicity Resources
www.olympus.net/okeefe/pubnet

Public Relations Society of America
www.hei.com/~prsa/history.html

Self-Promotion www.impulseresearch.com/impulse/resource.html

Standard Rate & Data Service www.srds.com

Ulrich's International Periodicals Directory
www.silverplatter.com/catalog/uigp.html

Appendix 8

Glossary of PR Terms

30 or ###. Indicates you've arrived at the end of the copy in a news release or story.

Ad. Short for advertising.

ADI. Area of Dominant Influence. An area in which a TV station has a large share of the viewing audience watching its program on a consistent basis.

Ad specialties. Items having the name/logo of your company to boost image awareness—mugs, pens, calendars, etc.

Ad value. The value of your placement (see definition for "Placement" following) if you had to purchase the space as an advertisement.

Advertising. Company messages in newspapers, on the radio or TV, paid for by the advertiser.

Advertorial. A paid advertisement that resembles a story. The advertorial is usually educational or instructional in nature, yet promotes the company message throughout.

Anchor. A person who hosts a TV news broadcast by giving news updates and introducing reporters with local, late-breaking or national/international news stories.

AP style. Associated Press style is the preferred method of presenting information for most newspapers.

Assignment editor. The person at a TV or radio station responsible for dispatching camera crews and reporters to cover news stories. Known as the "air traffic controller" of the station.

Associated Press (AP). A worldwide news-gathering agency encompassing more than 4,500 newspapers, and TV and radio stations around the globe.

Backgrounder. Usually part of a press kit, a backgrounder summarizes the history of a company, person, or current matter.

Banner. A large headline that runs across the entire page of a newspaper to attract the readers' attention. Newspapers compete for the best banners, because it may lead people to choose one newspaper to purchase over another.

Bartering. Swapping products or services of equal value. For example, a printer may barter with a marketing company.

Beat. A reporter's regular area of coverage and/or expertise, such as the courthouse or technical beat.

Blanketing. Sending one press release to a variety of media sources with no customization involved.

Body copy. All of the article except for the lead paragraph.

Bookending. A TV news term indicating the story begins and ends with a person.

Breaking news. News that is developing at the current moment; all details may not be in at that time.

Broadcast faxing/e-mailing. Using sophisticated software packages, a fax or e-mail can be created and programmed to go out to thousands with the click of a button.

B-roll. Basic footage of an event; not the finished TV story.

Byline. The name of the writer who wrote the story, found at the beginning or end of the story.

B&W. An acronym for black and white, meaning black and white photos supplied to newspapers or film provided to television.

Call letters. East of the Mississippi, the call letters for a broadcast station's name start with a W; west of the Mississippi, they start with K.

Camera cue light. A red light on the top/front of the camera indicating it is the one currently live or in use.

Canvassing. Calling a long list of media contacts after a broadcast fax has been sent out.

Caption. Also called a cutline, it is a few sentences describing an illustration or photograph.

Center spread. Two facing center pages, on one continuous page in a newspaper.

City desk. Where local news is processed.

Circulation. The total number of copies of the newspaper distributed to subscribers and news vendors in a single day.

Clip sheet. Filler material that newspapers use when they have nothing to fill the space.

Column. An article appearing regularly by the same writer or "columnist."

Consumer. One that utilizes economic goods and forms perceptions about you and your company. Anyone who uses your products or services directly or indirectly.

Copy editor. Usually the assistant to the city or national editor, the copy editor edits reporter's copy and write headlines.

CU. Close up. A broadcast term referring to a shot of an individual's face.

Cue. The signal to say or do something; usually to begin or end.

Cut. Also known as trim, when an editor decides to shorten a story to fit the space.

Dateline. Always precedes the first sentence of the lead, indicating the location and date of the story.

Day book. A computerized record of events to be covered by a media source that day/week. It includes the time, location, subject, and contact person.

Ears. Space at the top of the front page on each side of the paper's name; sometimes called a teaser because it may show an index to pages or feature stories.

Editor. The person responsible for deciding what news goes in the paper and where it will appear. Assigns and reviews stories submitted by staff reporters.

Editorial. A piece written by the newspaper's editors reflecting a point of view rather than hard news.

Exclusive. When you offer a hot story to only one media source because you feel they will give it the most play and attention.

Feature. A story that deals with something other than late-breaking news. If a house burns down, the time, date, and location is news. How people felt about it could be a feature.

Filler. A short, interesting, and sometimes humorous story an editor can use to fill space between longer articles.

Fringe time. The periods immediately before and after TV prime time, usually 4:30 p.m. to 7:30p.m. and after 11 p.m.

General assignment. A reporter who covers a variety of stories rather than focusing on one topic.

Glossy. A shiny, smooth photograph required to produce a sharp, clear reproduction on newsprint.

Green room. The room at the television station where you will wait to receive "the green light" to go on the air.

Headline. The few words over a story that summarize for the reader.

Hits. Meaning a media source has completed an interview and agreed to run a story.

Hook(s). The angle, the focus; what makes the story unique and different.

Hot. Your story is hot most particularly if it is timely, has an unusual hook, and appeals to a mass audience.

Inverted pyramid. A method of writing news stories in which the parts of the story are placed in descending order of importance.

Jump. The continuation of a story from one page to another, usually from outside to inside rather than to the same page.

Jumpline. The line that tells reader where the story jumps to.

Jumphead. The headline that helps people find the story they were reading on a previous page, that jumped to the inside.

Kill. To discard all or parts of the story before it is printed.

Lead. The first paragraph of a story, which usually contains the five "Ws"—or the who, what, when, where, and why.

Letters to the editor. Usually found opposite the editorial page, this section contains letters from readers expressing their opinions on stories published in the publication.

Logo. The graphic representation of your company.

Make-up. The arrangement of stories, headlines, pictures, and advertising on a page.

Marketing. Everything you do to get people to notice and patronize your business on a regular basis. PR is just one of the components of a good marketing plan. Other components include direct mail, advertising, telemarketing, and special events

Masthead. A publication's name, key people, address, and contact information, usually found on the editorial page.

Media kit. A collection of materials sent to an editor or reporter to help in writing a more complete story. Many times, media kits are distributed at a press conference. Also referred to as press kit.

Media list. A customized list of newspapers, radio, and TV station contacts to whom press releases are sent for the purposes of gaining publicity or goodwill.

Mug shot. A photo of a person's face only.

Multimedia. The combined use of media for maximum results including newspapers, magazines, billboards, radio, TV, etc.

National editor. Also called the wire editor, in charge of selecting and editing the news of the nation outside the newspaper's circulation area.

New media. Electronic Media, such as the Internet.

News hole. The place in a newspaper where only news, not advertising, appears.

Newspeg. The catchy, key element of any news story.

News services. Global news-gathering agencies, such as the Associated Press and the United Press International, that gather and distribute news to subscribing newspapers.

Newsworthy. Your story is newsworthy if it appeals to a mass audience, it fits the media source's format, and has a hook.

Niche. A specialization to which you and/or your company are an expert. For example, software for lawyers only; computer training for CEOs only.

Off the record. Information given to a reporter that is not supposed to be used for publication.

Op-ed page. Opinion editorial. The page on which reader's letters and opinions are printed.

Outdoor advertising. Can include but not limited to billboards, bus ads, yard signs, neon road signage, blimps, and balloons. Outdoor advertising can be bartered or sponsored cooperatively.

Penetration. The share of audience attention in a given area.

Photo release form. A signed permission slip to use name and photo in a story.

Pitch/pitching. Telephoning or discussing a story idea with a media source, using persuasive language.

Positioning. When placing a story, it's critical to communicate your message in a way that people will understand it as you *want* it understood. How you "position" the material allows you to succeed at this.

Press conference. A special event held to announce or clarify important information, where key resources might be available as a panel to answer questions from the media.

Press kit. A collection of materials sent to an editor or reporter to help in writing a more complete story. Many times, press kits are distributed at a press conference. The better name for it is a media kit.

Press release. Also called a news release or a media release. A carefully prepared arrangement of information to attract the press to write a story.

Prime time. When television has its largest audiences and highest advertising rates. Usually between 6:30 p.m.to 11 p.m. in most time zones.

Producer. In broadcast media, the person who assigns the stories and makes sure the segments are produced by deadline.

Proof. An impression of a printed page or story to be reviewed for errors before the final version is printed.

Proofreader. Someone who reads a proof and checks for punctuation and content errors.

Public relations. A discipline encompassing many activities all with the goal of creating a desired image with the public. It typically involves getting exposure in all types of media. For example, free stories and news about you and your company on an ongoing basis in newspapers, magazines, newsletters, radio, television, on Web sites, and other types of media that reach a wide audience.

Public service announcement (PSA). An announcement sent by a nonprofit organization only that is broadcast free of charge to promote programs, activities, or services.

Publisher. The chief executive officer and, many times, the owner of a newspaper or other publication.

Put to bed. The final steps taken before the presses start to run the papers.

Reuters. Founded in Great Britain in 1849, it's the first news gathering service in history.

ROP. Run of paper news and advertising. Means your story or ad will appear anywhere in the newspaper that is convenient for its layout.

Satellite media tour. A way to bring together people in a variety of different locations using sophisticated broadcast media equipment.

Shooter. The industry's nickname for a videographer or a photographer.

Sidebar. Related to a major story, it usually runs next to it to highlight information.

Sound bites. Words, or short phrases or a sentences that are typically colorful or clever, thus easily remembered and repeated by those that hear them.

Spin doctor. A nickname for a public relations expert that can put a "spin" on a crisis situation so it can be seen in a positive light.

Spot news. News information obtained first-hand.

Stringer. A part-time writer usually paid by the amount of copy delivered to an editor.

Talk show. A topic-oriented program involving experts on subjects of mass appeal

Target market. The specific group of people you want to reach with your message. The target market may be defined by demographics—young, upwardly mobile professionals with a $50,000 or higher household income; or by geographic area—individuals within a 20-minute drive of your business; or by any number of criteria.

Tear sheet. A sheet torn from a publication to prove insertion, usually of an advertisement. "Clips" are sheets torn of editorial material.

Teaser. A few catchy words usually found on the front of a newspaper to indicate an interesting story somewhere inside the publication.

Telephoto. The UPI service that transmits pictures to subscribing newspapers.

Timely. Meaning your story has a window of opportunity to run before it loses its interest factor. For example, a plane crashes and kills hundreds. A psychotherapist gets national attention for her role in treating not only the victims families.

Trends. A current style or preference. Paying attention to trends and how you and your company fit into those trends offers a window of opportunity for PR.

Typo. Short for typographical error, meaning a mistake made during the production of the story, not the writing of the story.

United Press International (UPI). One of several worldwide news services.

Video newspapers. On your TV, text screens advertising your event. Usually set to music. You can submit your text to the appropriate station. Usually four- to six-week lead time.

Wirephoto. The Associated Press service that transmits pictures to subscribing newspapers.

Index